W9-BTD-601

THE MAJOR THEMES OF ROBERT FROST

by James Radcliffe Squires

Ann Arbor
The University of Michigan Press

811

Copyright © by The University of Michigan 1963
All rights reserved
Library of Congress Catalog Card No. 63-9902
Published in the United States of America by
The University of Michigan Press and simultaneously
in Toronto, Canada, by Ambassador Books Limited
Manufactured in the United States of America
by Vail-Ballou Press, Inc., Binghamton, N.Y.

ACKNOWLEDGMENT is made of permission to quote from *Upper Pasture* by Charles Malam, © 1930, © renewed 1958, reprinted by permission of Holt, Rinehart and Winston, Inc.; from *Complete Poems of Robert Frost*, © 1916, 1921, 1923, 1928, 1930, 1935, 1939, 1943, 1944, 1945, 1947, 1948, 1951, 1956, 1958, 1962, reprinted by permission of Holt, Rinehart and Winston, Inc. and Laurence Pollinger Ltd.; from *In the Clearing* by Robert Frost, © 1951, 1962, reprinted by permission of Holt, Rinehart and Winston, Inc.; from *A Way Out* by Robert Frost, reprinted by permission of Holt, Rinehart and Winston, Inc.; from a letter of Robert Frost by his permission; from *The Letters of Ezra Pound*, reprinted by permission of Harcourt, Brace & World, Inc.; from *The Selected Letters of William James*, reprinted by permission of Paul R. Reynolds & Sons; and from *Collected Poems* and letters by Edward Thomas, reprinted by permission of Mrs. Helen Thomas.

FOR ARTHUR, NORMA, JOHN, AND HELEN
WITH WHOM EILEEN AND I SHARED THE
WATERS OF A WEST-RUNNING BROOK

The Major Themes of Robert Frost

PREFACE

Robert Frost recently remarked that the purpose of poetry is to express the ineffable. I gladly give over this task to the poet. For my own part I have in this book tried to speak about effable things. I have tried to concern myself with those aspects of Frost's work which will always make it valuable: its legality of language, its relevance to life, and above all its truth and honor of concept—the philosophic muse that speaks in the center of his poetry, giving, in the final analysis, intensity and endurance. These are effable things which will preserve Frost's literary reputation from large fluctuations and which even now within his lifetime spare the critic from having to argue his reputation. His poetry has carried the day, just as it will carry the centuries.

Some thanks and acknowledgments are in order. I am grateful to the College of Literature, Science, and the Arts at the University of Michigan for a leave of absence, and to the Horace H. Rackham School of Graduate Studies for a travel grant. Among the many friends who offered suggestions, I wish particularly to thank Mrs. Daniel Katz for bringing to my attention Charles Malam's poetry and Arthur Carr who told me about William James' correspondence with Henry Adams. Mr. and Mrs. Theodore Morrison also gave help.

Two of these chapters in somewhat different form were first given as public lectures. Chapter Three was delivered at Salonika, Greece, under the auspices of the United States Information Service; Chapter Seven at Western Reserve University in Cleveland, Ohio.

R. S.

CONTENTS

ONE

Grounds: Back and Fore

I

Robert Frost's elegant poetry stands alone. It is "modern" only in the sense that it is not Victorian or Georgian, as Ezra Pound immediately perceived when he saw *A Boy's Will* in London in 1913. But Frost's poetry is not modern in the sense that it is like any other poetry of the twentieth century. Not even in the matter of superficial form: diction, trope, technical versification.

I know of no satisfactory way of describing diction—unless by producing a concordance and cataloguing the most recurrent words. And such a method is cumbersome; if it delights the tree lovers, it disgusts the forest lovers. I shall earn the gratitude of neither by offering my impression that Frost's diction is by contemporary standards rather "pure." One seldom, perhaps never, finds Frost trying to re-establish the meaning of a word, either by unusual placement or by tampering with its components, or by illuminating the frightened pun which squirms in many English words. He is not, to mention extreme examples, Dylan Thomas or E. E. Cummings. No, the dictionary meanings will suffice.

As to device, while Frost, like other contemporaries, leans hardest on metaphor and simile, his ambition is comparatively restricted. The mackerel spawn which Yeats observed as a boy becomes the basis for "the mackerel-crowded seas," yet the implications for Yeats eventually convert the image away from anything usual to something extraordinary and symbolic. I should say that Frost's images, though they have overtones of suggestion, first serve the demands of sensory experience before those of any symbolic scheme. Realism—even when the metaphor deftly implies that the reality is rather more lovely or sad or complex than we had thought before. And so, allowing for an important exception here or there, one may expect Frost's metaphors to exist hardly at all for the purpose of some grand scheme or epistemology and, indeed, to exist more for the line in which they occur than for the whole poem. One does not feel in Frost's images that strange spiritual seeding which one may feel in Yeats's, along with the sensation of dumb tendrils moving out into half-apprehended margins. Instead, one feels a hand close completely upon an object; an eye, an ear take it in.

As to versification, Frost is no innovator in a period primarily devoted to experimentation. Think of all the boring utterances about a "new music," which the century has produced. Or think of the radical movement in the prosody of the greatest innovator (as well as the greatest bore) of them all, Ezra Pound. True, I read occasionally that some of Frost's poems are imitations of Latin meters which the ears of the initiated readily recognize. One hates not be be initiated, but I submit that these experiments are as doubtful as Tennyson's experiments in classical meter, and that they sound no different from his other poems. To my ear, all Frost's poetry is essentially iambic, and while one can readily agree with him when he says he writes his "own kind of blank verse," neither the statement nor the agreement suggests that the form aspires to anything new. On the contrary, just as Frost assumes that language is a specific inheritance rather than a fortune to be made anew for each generation, so he assumes that versification is an inarguable science, a knowledge to be put to specific use rather than an ulterior means of seeking knowledge.

For Frost form has almost no other reward than itself. Hence his often repeated statement (repeated as much by himself as others) to the effect that he would as lief write a poem in free verse as play tennis without a net. Despite the owlishness of the words, I am not tempted to reply. The statement seems to me to say little about poetry in general but much about Frost's particular poetry. Form to him is not mystagogy; it is fun. It is separable from content, a source of amusement in itself. This is hardly to say that he is unconcerned with appropriateness or taste in his choice and execution. He is wholeheartedly concerned, but essentially because it is part of the fun, the game, the puzzle. For this reason one may in some of Frost's poems feel a disappointment that though there is a shift of meaning or attitude the poem jogs on as if it had not heard what it was saying. But also for this reason one may quite as often feel that in no other modern poet does the whole poem finally remain so whole, turning with all the spare, wicked grace of true epigram. In this way, and in this way only, does it seem possible to say of Frost that there is something "classical" about his poems, for such wholeness does allow one a mirage-glimpse of what appears to be an antique ease of relationship between poet and environment. In the end, the content of Frost's poetry destroys the illusion.

In another and larger way Frost is separate from the modern poet. When I try to define this way, everything goes shimmery and delicate. I sense the difference, the outlines tantalize, and yet I am not sure that I can gather together all the important things. Still, it seems better to try than to protect myself.

The whole form of Frost's knowledge is different from that of the typical contemporary. If one were to delineate the typical modern poet who has been writing and publishing since, say, 1930, he would be obliged to devote much of the portrait not to the materials of the poet, for these vary greatly, but to the attitude toward the materials. The typical modern poet writes a poem in which his consciousness, his presence, is less than fully committed to what he is writing about. One is aware of content while at the same time aware that the poet in some ghostly manner flakes away from the stuff of his composition and stands preserved and intact. Neither the poet nor the poem gains the upper hand. Such, for example, is the final effect of W. H. Auden's poetry. There are probably a number of causes, but one stands out as basic. The typical modern does not, or does not wish to, believe in his environment. The surrealist fragments the world about him. The idealist thinks of existence and the poem as a time capsule filled with the gorgeous colors of ephemeral experience buried in the darkness of a skull. But whether we regard the beautiful extremes of Dylan Thomas or Wallace Stevens, whether we think of the poet in Wales or Hartford, Connecticut, again and again we are aware of the poet who finds the world either too strange or repulsive for final belief. So that his belief finally centers in himself as the container of that world.

If, as I believe, none of this is true of Robert Frost's poetry, what is the reason? If there is a primary reason it is that the typical modern poet has drawn his subjects not from the City of God but from the city of man, from something that is today continuously failing. It was all very well for Samuel Johnson to believe utterly in London—nay, one street in London was enough—for nothing of that world could change. But today one sees mainly that affluence and justice and freedom do not make man good or wise or happy. While the voices of good will and reason are mocked in the lurid fifth acts of history, which come upon us again and again, the four preceding acts are forgotten. I do not say that Frost is unaware of all this. He is sadly aware. But between him and the fifth act stands a world of extensive, if incomplete, order which he can balance against the abnormal prodigies of civilization. You put in the seed, you cultivate, you reap, all in the sane relationship of the grand cause and the grand effect, all in direct relationship with life as it was once more happily conceived. You stand in the good of the senses and seasons. You see man in the perspective not of history but of nature which has, surely, a half-life of infinity.

Such a view may, of course, amount to provincialism. But so, just as surely, does being tethered to the self-torturing consciousness of the twentieth-century metropolis—as is neatly illustrated in the recent rather painful remarks of Lionel Trilling about Frost's poetry. How long it took Trilling to see Frost's greatness—or to use a word like the one which embarrassed Frost—to see the "terror" of his poetry. But, of course, one must say that Trilling's long immunity came from the provincialism of the city. And the most telling effect of this kind of provincialism for such as Trilling or W. H. Auden has not been cosmopolitan smugness but the opposite, the thinness of the armor. I think now of a whole generation whose moral and political goals (though perhaps not the ideals) have had to change drastically. From Marx to Christ or to a sterile conservatism. To take an example for its near convenience, is one to wonder that Mr. Trilling's short stories—orderly, humane, and beautiful—deal with moral situations which they cannot resolve and with a reality which finally is made unreal by multiple symbols?

I hope no one will say that I am sponsoring a back-to-the-soil movement or even a down-with-Auden-and-Trilling movement. I am concerned only with suggesting how Frost's sources of knowledge and feeling separate him from those who have taken a road more traveled by. Indeed, while it is clear that Frost's position has given him certain distinct advantages—a clear confidence in what he has to say and a superlative realism —one hardly supposes that the position has been without disadvantage. One may feel at times that the clear confidence becomes smugness or that the reality becomes oversimplification. And perhaps there is some loss of psychological power, at least in one narrow way. Frost, of course, very evidently has felt his separation from other poets and has as a matter of fact worked at preserving it. Even as a young man, as he told me once, when it was hard for him to find a publisher, he had the feeling that William Vaughn Moody's interest in his poetry was a dangerous one, that he wanted "to take him over." So, too, later with Ezra Pound. He has preserved an independence at the price of isolating himself from the company of poets. I am not saying that he has not known many poets, but I believe that except for Edward Thomas his profounder friendships have been with scholars, teachers, and the laity.

[5]

Indeed, some of the things I have heard Frost say about other contemporary poets are so naughty, even though funny, as to be shocking.

Perhaps because of his calculated and enforced separation and for the reason that he no doubt finds his way superior (which inspires Frost's puckish, touch-me-not behavior), a reviewer in a high-brow literary magazine once wrote that Frost had a "hatred of the young poet." The language seems strong, and I would change "hatred" to something like "affectionate contempt." But whether hatred or contempt, a rejection is there, and it has cut him away from whatever is going on at the tips of the bough. A good deal of blight is no doubt going on, but also growth. His own poetry then has been separated from one great source of renewal, even though it is open to question whether Frost's conservative aesthetic would under any circumstances have changed. Yeats, while suspicious and jealous of the young Eliot and Pound, learned from them. He learned how to become a greater poet than his early poems suggested he could.

Of some importance, though whether great or small is hard to say, has been the effect of this disassociation upon Frost the public figure. One gathers from Elizabeth Sergeant's very good biography that Frost by temperament was as a young man a shy person, easily wounded and proud, as well as touched by stage fright. These traits disappear with his success as a poet, and the well-known platform personality emerges with its teasing asides and country-store philosophy. Let me agree at once that there is something lovable about this personality. But one ought not to take Frost's public maunderings for final wisdom; a form of humor, perhaps, a graceful, fortuitous intuition, yes, but they are in general only quizzical fiddling without hard thought or development behind them. I worry even more. Upon occasion, fortunately rare, the facile generalizations pass as conclusion in the lesser poems. No one has a right even to want to change the life of another, particularly of one who has given great treasure to the world. But sometimes one wishes that Frost had cut out some of that arch kidding around and saved some of the poems that he only half-wrote before he threw them to the gallery.

II

When Pound wrote to Alice Corbin Henderson in March 1913 about Frost, he described him as "VURRY Amur'k'n, with I think, the seeds of grace." The seeds germinated well, but I am not at all sure that the implied opposition between grace and Frost's being very American is valid. To be sure, Pound is being Pound the funny-letter-writer, and what he probably had in mind was Frost's settings and his distaste for artiness. Yet, if Frost does not fit in well with modern American or British poets, he fits in with an American pattern of the New Englander. It may be that Hippolyte Taine worked his theory of the effect of climate on literature a bit hard, but it would be foolish to suppose that environment is without an effect, even a profound effect sometimes.

There is a greater continuity, a braver changelessness about New England than about any other part of America. As is easily gathered from Frost's poem "New Hampshire," New England is virtually useless except to look at. Deserted textile mills, old foundations latticed with blackberry canes, diminished towns where no new houses have been built in a hundred years and where the town square and chapel speak from another century. The scenery is always a bit melancholy. The cut-over land is serried with sapling and steeplebush. The great autumns for all their brilliance and clarity are nevertheless solemn, as are the oases of pure wilderness before one stumbles into a slab lumbering road which goes somewhere. The winter is as indomitable a presence as the old Puritan conscience. Yet New England does not have dramatic scenery. Despite Emerson's lines, "The God who made New Hampshire / Taunted the lofty land / With little men," New England neither dwarfs nor magnifies people. But it demands much of them while

[7]

giving little, leaving them with a resolve to save their breath with each other, though forcing them to brood in isolation or to find in the land the herb heartsease—as Hawthorne in the story "The Ambitious Guest" well knew. In truth the New England heart both broods and creates, paradoxically combining an outward frugality with an inner prodigality. Thoreau, saving his soul so as to spend it.

To be both frugal and prodigal is to be rich, or at least it enables one to feel rich—to be proud in poverty, even foolishly so, to be absolutely certain of what is right, even absurdly so. This is the prime source of the weird optimism which characterizes Ralph Waldo Emerson. It is well and proper to relate Emerson's transcendentalism to German idealism and to a reaction against the frown of Calvinism. But Emerson goes further than his antecedents and counterparts. He felt after meeting Coleridge, Wordsworth, and Carlyle in 1832 that "not one of these is a mind of the very first class." He does not tell us his reasons, but it is possible to guess that among them might be the way in which these Englishmen (who had, surely, altogether first-class minds) viewed nature. Though nature might for Coleridge participate in Gothic moods or for Wordsworth reflect a personal guilt or joy, for all three it meant essentially a source of peace and healing, separate if not clearly differentiated from man's turbulence or perversity. For Emerson, nature is not *symbolic* of the good and beautiful. It calls these things up for him, not because it gives omens or intimations of immortality but because it is in Emerson's mind *identical* with them. There is no difference. As he writes in *Nature:* ". . . every natural process is a version of a moral sentence. The moral law lies at the centre of nature and radiates to the circumference." To believe this is to be not only rich but, as almost everyone else in the world has gleefully pointed out, an incurable optimist—or, as a few have darkly hinted, to have no sense of the evil in the universe. Whether the metaphysics be bad or not, the state is enviable. And perhaps impossible to attain today. Even so, something of Emerson's optimism comes into Frost's poetry—not necessarily from Emerson, though Frost has greatly admired his poetry, but from the equivalence of their New England tempers. In both, the poetry and thought more often than not turn pretty much from the tight-lipped and tight-fisted people of their world to converse with nature itself. As Emerson wrote in "Fate":

> Delicate omens traced in air
> To the lone bard true witness bare;
> Birds with auguries on their wings
> Chanted undeceiving things,
> Him to beckon, him to warn;
> Well might then the poet scorn
> To learn of scribe or courier
> Hints writ in vaster character;
> And on his mind, at dawn of day,
> Soft shadows of the evening lay.
> For the prevision is allied
> Unto the thing so signified;
> Or say, the foresight that awaits
> Is the same Genius that creates.

Nature, as a matter of fact, often takes up the rôle deserted by human beings in the poetry of Frost and Emerson. Compare, for example, the flirtatious bird in Frost's "The Woodpile" with the bird in Emerson's "The Titmouse." Emerson's bird:

> Sped, when I passed his sylvan fort,
> To do the honours of his court,
> As fits a feathered lord of land;
> Flew near, with soft wing grazed my hand,
> Hopped on the bough, then, darting low,
> Prints his small impress on the snow,
> Shows feats of his gymnastic play,
> Head downward, clinging to the spray.

Although the last four lines could pass for Frost's, there is a pervasive difference between the two poets. Because Emerson so unequivocally believed that the moral world and nature were one and the same, he does not very often bother to detail nature—the moral statement serves the same purpose. For the same reason, the philosophical optimist does not, if nature and moral law are one, need to be instructed by nature. He is instructed by the fact of being part of it. He may not even feel much need to bring a poem to a particular conclusion. The conclusion is implicit in the parts, the atmosphere. Indeed, the ultimate extension of Emerson's belief contradicts writing poetry at all.

But Frost is neither a professional philosopher nor a total optimist. His poems work through detail; they come to specific conclusions. For all his evident relationship to Emerson, the relationship makes better sense when one considers his poetry also in relationship with two other New England poets, Emily Dickinson and Edwin Arlington Robinson.

Emily Dickinson could never have publicly stated the observations which she made in her poetry. They do not belong to the domestic scene, the Sunday school class, or to any civil rendezvous. They belong to life, these awful and sudden and oblique views, yet they represent neither a "higher truth" nor a "lower truth." They are intensely beautiful but intensely insane, and, excepting that the experiencer be a poet, neither ought nor can be given words. Granting all this and granting Emily Dickinson her New England atmosphere which encouraged an inner life while discouraging its public expression, one understands especially well both her urgency to write and her reticence to publish. In all her lovely, hard virginity, her grand isolation, she turns like many another New England poet to expressing herself not merely through nature but almost as if she were expressing herself to nature. So presumptuously perfect does this communication become that in the end she writes a poetry of primitive superstition. Like a

savage, she takes as personally directed what happens in nature
—the snake, the buzzing fly. Whereas Emerson identifies
nature with an abstract idea Dickinson totemistically identifies
it with a mood, a desire, a fear.

Both Emerson and Dickinson assume that direct communication with human beings is unlikely and in their separate ways
commandeer nature in some substantive manner. Edwin Arlington Robinson, however, narrows his focus to the incommunication itself. The difficulty of communication is sometimes thought
of as a modern problem or theme, but it seems to have been
implicit in New England for at least a century. Consider only
the difficulty of confession, the disguised faces, the secrets in
Hawthorne's work. Robinson over and over again indicates how
luxuriantly the hidden pressure grows in the solitary inner lives
of his New Englanders, bursting forth at last in some exotic
and surprising way; a way which is really dramatic gesture
rather than expression: the suicide of Richard Cory or Mr.
Flood's schizoid conversation. Concentrating on the isolation
of the soul, Robinson, alone among his New England com-
patriots, is hardly concerned with nature. At most it constitutes
setting. It is never one of the *dramatis personae*. It is never
law, never the equivalent of the inner state.

Robert Frost's poetry partakes of all these attitudes, modify-
ing each to the others. Like Thoreau he begins with the consciousness of a rich spiritual life which is difficult to share.
Seeking like Emerson for an abstract basis in his communion
with nature he seems almost able to posit what Emerson wrote
in "The Humble-Bee":

> ... Nature ever faithful is
> To such as trust her faithfulness.
> When the forest shall mislead me,
> When the night and morning lie,
> When sea and land refuse to feed me
> 'Twill be time enough to die;

Then will yet my mother yield
A pillow in her greenest field,
Nor the June flowers scorn to cover
The clay of their departed lover.

But Frost will not go quite this far, for there is always the impression that perhaps nature is faithful only to herself.

Like Emily Dickinson, Frost seems at times to write a poetry of superstition—ironically a sophisticated evolution of transcendental attitudes, but he almost always ends by denying the superstition as fantasy. Dickinson never denies, although sometimes she seems austerely amused at her own portentousness.

Finally, like Robinson, Frost is appreciative of the New England disease of incommunication. He has some devastatingly lonely poems. Unlike Robinson, however, he tends to leave the inner loneliness pure, unresolved by dramatic act. Or, he devises monologues and soliloquies which publish the rich findings of a life, as in the particularly fine poem "The Black Cottage."

My point is simple. Frost's genius is impressively evident in the versatility of his poetry. It has the breadth and ideal passion of Emerson's, the ikons and incantation of Dickinson's, the pathetic irony of Robinson's. Furthermore, because at its best it has all of these things together, Frost's poetry is greater than Emerson's, Dickinson's or Robinson's. Frost becomes so superbly the New England poet that one is not tempted to call him one.

III

Frost has evoked no school of poetry, but to say so may only be a way of saying that Yeats and Eliot are easier to imitate. They are easier certainly to parody, for their poems are produced in the extremes of reaction and diction, whereas Frost is happiest in moderation. At any rate, while it is true that there is no school of Frost, he has had some effect on some poets. One glances at them not for what they may reveal about modern poetry but for what they reveal about Frost's poetry. They help to illuminate it and to define its true shape. I think at the moment of two poets, one well known, the other obscure, Edward Thomas and Charles Malam.

Frost met Edward Thomas in 1913 in England at a time when Thomas felt played out and at loose ends. He had written too many books for too little money. His bibliography shows that in 1911 he published five books, in 1912 four books, and four more in 1913. The trouble with most of his prose books is that they are neither good nor bad, than which nothing could be more tiring or more depressing for a man of very evident genius. His friendship with Robert Frost and his admiration for Frost's poetry seem to have freed him from bondage. He suddenly wrote what he essentially wished to write, poems rather than charming and respectable essays about other writers or the English countryside. In 1916, when he was nearing forty, his first poems were published. He died on a French battlefield in 1917, and most of his poems were published posthumously.

Many of Thomas' poems show an influence from Frost, but it is an influence of method rather than attitude. Thomas wrote narrative poems, for example, involving country characters, wherein it is evident that he was trying to capture a use of dialect which he admired in Frost's poetry. He wrote in 1915 to Gordon Bottomley, "All [Frost] insists on is what he believes he finds in all poets—absolute fidelity to the postures which the voice assumes in the most expressive intimate speech." But the important things he learned from Frost's poetry were not speech rhythms but how to write about nature without prettification, how to bring the inherent materials of the poem to a climactic shift and how to extract from observation alone the daimon of poetry. One short example will demonstrate all of these features. The poem "Thaw" reminds one of Frost. It is, I believe, as good as anything Frost himself ever did in such a narrow scope:

[13]

Over the land freckled with snow half-thawed
The speculating rooks at their nests cawed
And saw from elm-tops, delicate as flower of grass,
What we below could not see, Winter pass.

At such levels Thomas will often remind one of Frost while seeming somewhat purer, seeming to distil the idiom more patiently. In his poem "The Barn," the thatch roof has been spoiled by the drip from an elm. The poem finishes:

Starlings used to sit there with bubbling throats
Making a spiky beard as they chattered
And whistled and kissed, with heads in air,
Till they thought of something else that mattered.

But now they cannot find a place,
Among all those holes, for a nest any more.
It's the turn of lesser things, I suppose.
Once I fancied 'twas starlings they built it for.

Now, in these lines one may readily feel the authority of Frost in the nice snubnosed plainness of "something else that mattered." Or in the little colloquial down turn of "I suppose." And in the shrug of pleasant, egoistic pathos in both the rhythm and statement of the last line. But the poem has a different kind of audacity from that which Frost would have given it in the combination of lines: "And whistled and kissed with heads in air,/ Till they thought of something else that mattered." These lines work the quatrain toward a delicate tension which at base is sexual. Frost always looks the other way when nature is breeding.

One can feel that had Thomas lived his poetry might have asserted its individuality and that in certain respects have become a more broadly sophisticated poetry than Frost's. Even so, it would not, I believe, ever have developed the ultimate strength of Robert Frost's work. Here is what I mean. Thomas writes in "When First":

When first I came here I had hope,
Hope for I knew not what. Fast beat
My heart at sight of the tall slope
Of grass and yews . . .

The poem continues on to record that though hope is gone love

Will grow, and louder the heart's dance
At parting than at meeting be.

The poem remains entirely autobiographical. It is Thomas' hope, his love. It never becomes a poem about love or hope. Frost, on the other hand, even when one is most acutely aware of direct experience in the poem, moves inevitably toward a theme. His poems always broaden. It is entirely to the point to observe that Thomas wrote on May 22, 1915, to Eleanor Farjeon:

I like your rainbow, but mine that I saw with Frost seems like the first that ever was except that I knew it was a rainbow. I can't imagine a painter interfering with either. Mine was too much of a pure rainbow, a new toy discovered by Apollo, for anyone to paint. It was more for a mythologist clad in skins.

To anticipate the point: Thomas cannot imagine interfering with the rainbow. Frost knows exactly how to interfere. Years later he published "Iris by Night" which obviously treats the episode Thomas refers to:

One misty evening, one another's guide,
We two were groping down a Malvern side...
There came a moment of confusing lights,
Such as according to belief in Rome
Were seen of old at Memphis on the heights
Before the fragments of a former sun
Could concentrate anew and rise as one.
Light was a paste of pigment in our eyes.

[15]

And then there was a moon and then a scene
So watery as to seem submarine;
In which we two stood saturated, drowned. . . .
Then a small rainbow like a trellis gate
A very small moon-made prismatic bow,
Stood closely over us through which to go.
And then we were vouchsafed the miracle
That never yet to other two befell
And I alone of us have lived to tell.
A wonder! Bow and rainbow as it bent,
Instead of moving with us as we went,
(To keep the pots of gold from being found)
It lifted from its dewy pediment
Its two mote-swimming many-colored ends,
And gathered them together in a ring.
And we stood in it softly circled round
From all division time or foe can bring
In a relation of elected friends.

The point now is surely clear. Though the poem is given to
a description of a phenomenon, though one understands from
the outset that it all happened, at the end neither the rainbow
nor the characters are so important as the sudden light, however iridescent that light is, which hovers about not the fact
but the idea of friendship. The poem is an earnest lesson in
how object becomes subject in superior poetry—and without
losing actuality. This was the one lesson that Edward Thomas
did not learn from Robert Frost. I do not think it can be
learned even though it is easily seen. If it could be learned
there would be no minor poets—only good or bad major poets.
Of the other poet, Charles Malam, I know little other
than that he knew Frost and was encouraged by him. His
book *Upper Pasture* was published in 1930. The influence of
Frost begins with the title itself and pervades the whole book.
And one feels about the book as about Edward Thomas'

poetry, that it is difficult to sound anything like Frost without sounding too much like him. But Thomas could upon occasion rise above this difficulty, largely because he could bring a different scene and insight to a technique. Charles Malam could not. My intention is certainly not to make fun of Malam, who strikes me as a better poet than many who win prizes today, but to use a poem or two as a gauge of Frost's greatness. Two poems will suffice. First, "Stars":

> It was so vast a thing to see
> A universe poured recklessly
> Over the floor of Cosmic space
> To comfort and to quiet me.
>
> There was not left the smallest place
> But had its star and, like fine lace
> Seeming to be yet not to be,
> Bore in its bit the pattern's trace.
>
> Above I saw it, and around,
> And where the edges touched the ground
> A light that may have been the Face
> Shone through. And there was not a sound.

The final sentence is the only one that might not pass for at least bad Frost. But that last line! One feels the poem, all its illumination, all its heart, had nowhere after all to go. And worse, one feels a talent has been cheated by an overpowering admiration for another poet. Another example, the poem "Burdens."

> Lying in the pungent moss
> On elbow and knee
> I saw an ant carrying
> A crumb large as three

And felt the earth pushing up—
And saw with grim mirth
A poet in the mint-moss
Carrying the earth,

I by my aching body
Knowing I must be
As heavy to the green earth
As earth was to me!

Here one cannot but be discomfited by the memory of Frost's poem "To Earthward," and not the least of the discomfort is the awareness that everything in the poem becomes inappropriately subjective and tricky in the second quatrain.

No, Frost's poetry could never produce a school, for it is like an element with which little else will blend or alloy. Edward Thomas must have been much like Frost in some part of his essential self, and one can be glad that Frost helped him to speak. This is a literary accident. It will not be duplicated.

But why does Frost's poetry overwhelm a poet like Charles Malam? The answer lies less in the nature of Frost's poetry than in the kind of temperament attracted to the poetry. Such a temperament is stirred by nature in an essentially romantic way—there is perhaps no other way to be *stirred* by nature. Such a temperament is looking for a resolution of personal problems in the assumedly vaster, truer, and more objective scope of nature. But Frost never resolves a personal problem; indeed, his poetry almost entirely pretends that he has no personal problem. Temperaments like Charles Malam's want really to go back to Wordsworth and should, for therein is a great untapped reservoir of possibility, as great as the century has found in John Donne. But the choice is not really between Frost the modern and Wordsworth the antique. It is between Wordsworth and Browning. For like Browning's, Frost's poetry tends to try to create beauty out of materials not really beautiful in themselves. Extraordinary gardens with ordinary toads in them. Frost's poetry is a careful disguise of personality, a creation of not an exotic mask but a blunt face of ordinariness. That is why I must distrust most of the anecdotal "biographies" of Frost. They are true lies.

I know of only one place where the worldly face is cast aside. It is in a letter to Edward Thomas' widow. If one were to write a biography of Robert Frost he would have to begin with it and from such a beginning work far and deep into the complex of sentiment and austerity of his subject. I do not plan a biography, but here is the letter.

Amherst, Massachusetts,
April 27th, 1917

People have been praised for self-possession in danger. I have heard Edward doubt if he was as brave as the bravest. But who was ever so completely himself right up to the verge of destruction, so sure of his thought, so sure of his word? He was the bravest and best and dearest man you and I have ever known. I knew from the moment when I first met him at his unhappiest that he would someday clear his mind and save his life. I have had four wonderful years with him. I know he has done this all for you: he is yours. But you must let me cry my cry for him as if he were *almost* all mine too.

Of the three ways out of here, by death where there is no choice, by death where there is a noble choice, and by death where there is a choice not so noble, he found the greatest way. There is no regret: nothing that I will call a regret. Only I can't help wishing he could have saved his life without so wholly losing it and come back from France not too much hurt to enjoy our pride in him. I want to see him to tell him something. I want to tell him, what I think he liked to hear from me, that he was a poet. I want to tell him that I love those he loved and hate those he hated. (But the hating will wait: there will be a time for hate.) I had meant to talk endlessly with him still, either here in our mountains or, as I had found my longing was more and more, there at Leddington where we first talked of war.

It was beautiful as he did it. And I don't suppose there is anything for us to do to show our admiration but to love him forever.

It is well to remember this letter as one moves on to Frost's poems, through his shield of triple bronze.

TWO

Weather: Inner and Outer

I

One finds it easy to suppose that Robert Frost has always been able to make the kind of poem for which he has been readily admired: the horse, the snow, the dark woods—all in a clear congruency, yet squeezed like clay until allegories of grief and joy spread from between the fingers. To do this is to contain and transform the environment, to make a permanent predicate of what merely happens. It is, ultimately, to conquer nature in the formalities of a drama where man faces some manner of temptation: he is tempted to disappear in the dark woods; he is tempted to climb to heaven. In effect, the temptation is only mildly perverse, mildly self-destructive. The resistance to the temptation is, however, of some intensity, and the triumph lies in refusing to give up any degree of being human in order to become more natural. There is something odd in the triumph, for the conqueror and the conquered, man and nature, are assumed to be conspirators. They have an agreement. They mirror each other.

If the triumph is sly, the desire for the triumph, for the conspiracy, the arrangement, is not. Man has more often than not desired this conspiracy between himself and his outer world. The desire links the metaphysical poet of the seventeenth century with the romantic rhapsodist. Donne's twin compasses and Shelley's Mont Blanc derive from a similar urgency to find in the external nature which defines, contrasts, and opposes a liaison which co-ordinates and affirms. Admirable. Still one must observe that though most of Frost's readers feel that this is the formula which Frost over and over again exploits in his poems, in all reality and in spite of his instinctive desire he contrives this easy unity of man and nature in only a handful of poems, and these poems are not quite his best. The desire may be imperious, but his ability to look upon nature as a friendly mirror is limited to those poems where he is content to do little other than represent nature, to see it intimately, often tenderly, but not to attempt to understand, only to record. This is not to say that Frost does ill to write such a poem. "Blue-Butterfly Day," for example, strikes me as a neglected little masterpiece, as minor and brilliant as Dürer's pieces of sod. The reader must utterly accept the blue butterflies which we are told are:

> flowers that fly and all but sing:
> And now from having ridden out desire
> They lie closed over in the wind and cling
> Where wheels have freshly sliced the April mire.

We are not likely to get a better poetry of observation. It is consummate because of Frost's ability to create, when he will, from experience, which, while depending on the senses, cannot be described as sensuous. There is no impression of the egotistical observer's being important, so that such a poem as "Blue-Butterfly Day" asserts the illusion of being less an observation than a thing in the world, a self. No doubt this great strength in Frost's poetry derives in part from his instinctive insistence on narrowing his poems of observation to one kind of sensation at a time. If he is concerned with the sound of the scythe he largely emphasizes the experience of the ear. If he is concerned with color, then sound and touch are diminished. We neither expect nor find a synesthetic confusion of sensations.

Not all his simple poems are poems of observation, and these require a different narrowing. In "Going for Water," a young couple whose well has gone dry must seek a brook in the woods at night:

> We ran as if to meet the moon
> That slowly dawned behind the trees,

The barren boughs without the leaves,
  Without the birds, without the breeze.

But once within the wood, we paused
  Like gnomes that hid us from the moon,
Ready to run to hiding new
  With laughter when she found us soon.

Each laid on other a staying hand
  To listen ere we dared to look,
And in the hush we joined to make
  We heard, we knew we heard the brook.

A note as from a single place,
  A slender tinkling fall that made
New drops that floated on the pool
  Like pearls, and now a silver blade.

This poem is of a different order from "Blue-Butterfly Day."
The viewpoint is complicated by being dual; the poem is not
primarily one of sight or sound. Yet it is a very consciously
limited poem. For the environment is severed from any suggestion of a surrounding world. Or say, this poem assumes that
the observable world consists of three objects: a dry well, a
moonlit woods and a brook, nothing else. The oversimplification
gets to heaven through the exportable veracity of the final
quatrain. This brook is a small, lonely god, awaiting with grave
dignity our witness. No mere concentration, no mere intensifica-
tion, this apotheosis subdues all other elements. It is a method
of limiting.

A similar deification of an object powers the lathe in "The
Runaway." Human sympathy, pity, humor, and pride inter-
weave. And yet . . . and yet the world is but a little world, and
the focus of attention shapes a divinity:

[23]

A little Morgan had one forefoot on the wall,
The other curled at his breast. He dipped his head
And snorted at us. And then he had to bolt.
We heard the miniature thunder where he fled,
And we saw him, or thought we saw him, dim and grey,
Like a shadow against the curtain of falling flakes.
'I think the little fellow's afraid of the snow.
He isn't winter-broken. It isn't play
With the little fellow at all. He's running away.
I doubt if even his mother could tell him, "Sakes,
It's only weather." He'd think she didn't know!
Where is his mother? He can't be out alone.'
And now he comes again with clatter of stone,
And mounts the wall again with whited eyes
And all his tail that isn't hair up straight.
He shudders his coat as if to throw off flies.
'Whoever it is that leaves him out so late,
When other creatures have gone to stall and bin,
Ought to be told to come and take him in.'

Make no mistake. This kind of poetry has a spirit as primitive as magic. No matter what the human observer says, no matter how much the words seem like local color, one only takes the words as an attempt to contain a god. At the same time the wildness of the god, his miniature thunder, escape containment, and in a sudden bouleversement the god seems the cryptic observer rather than the observed. We speak then both truly and sarcastically when we say that the poem is perfectly self-contained. We speak best when we note that the poem presents inarguable authority, the authority which comes from having been there and seen and—even more important—from having been seen. Indeed, this complex authority is at the heart of Frost's seemingly simple powers of observation.

Even so, this very authority makes for Frost an exquisite discontent. The truth is that Frost has not been quite satisfied with what the eye can see when focused briefly, determinedly, within very small purlieus . . . and no questions asked. He has found in the long run that he cannot keep from looking farther than the immediate object and that when he does so, the environment opens upon a bewilderment of landscapes with questions rising like mist. And he has had to parley with these questions, which can be answered not by repeating what he has seen in nature within a limited frame of perception, but only by drifting out among the mists and guessing the way. He sees complexity, inhuman mysteries in nature, and still he desires to find himself the microcosmos of nature. To so see and to so desire has forced Frost to lengthen his poetry, to stretch it from the arresting simplicity of "Blue-Butterfly Day" or the arrested simplicity of "The Runaway" to more intricate conceivings— and what is much more grave to discover in himself and in man generally a complexity to match that of nature. This stretching, which can be described as a growth, is not, however, exactly chronological. That is to say, the early poems are not simple and the later ones complex. Rather, his thought moves back and forth continuously. His poems stop the pendulum at certain arbitrary points. But since the movement itself is perennial, perpetual, he has found it expedient to divide nature into three sorts—the intimate nature of "Blue-Butterfly Day," the outer nature of the lengthened landscape which finally includes intangible galaxies, and, finally, the continuously elongated, searching nature of man, reaching toward both the near and the far nature outside himself. In the division the questions involving relationships between them all arise. And it is to these questions that the most important poems pay attention. Yet the questions, and hence the important poems, are rooted in Frost's apprehension of a discrepancy between an inner or intimate nature and an outer or remote nature.

II

Who would quarrel with the statement that Robert Frost appears to be at his happiest and most comfortable when he turns to direct, spontaneous observation of relatively natural things in an environment which seems writ large? After all, he has proclaimed himself an "environmentalist." One thinks of the domestic temperature of "The Pasture," the stunning simplicity of the little calf so young it totters when its mother licks it. "The Pasture," of course, and other relatively affirmative poems belong to that very work which has brought to Frost a general popularity. A popularity both with women's clubs and school boys—the one not too easy to come by, the other almost impossible. There is no harm in general popularity, nor do I see any reason for attempting to rescue Frost from ladies and school boys. I intend no treachery to him or them in suggesting that these poems are misrepresentative in that they deliberately stop short of the problems which underlie Frost's whole poetic life. They belong, to be sure, in the body of Frost's poetry and as representatives of his intimacy with nature they are valuable, but one's assessment needs to be tempered by a contrast with his two other kinds of nature poetry—first, the kind of poem where to the degree that it tends to desert direct observation it tends to recreate nature. And, secondly, the kind where Frost beholds not genial amity but grim goddesses in the temple of nature.

"The Demiurge's Laugh" is a good place to begin such a contrast. It is a rewarding poem and particularly noteworthy since it is among his early poems. It begins with the characteristic scenic-experiential assuredness which marks much of Frost's poetry. He is "far in the sameness of the wood." (Could anyone but Frost extract so much from the word "sameness"?) But the poem swiftly substitutes for the ordinary character of woods an entirely extraordinary one. Chasing an answer to an unexpressed question (though the reader assumes that the question involves "the riddle of nature"), the poet discovers that he has been pursuing a false god and indeed that he has even passed beyond the object of his search—Demiurge (the Platonic complex of a heartless creator and destroyer), for the god rises "from his wallow" and laughs a laugh which shows that he "utterly couldn't care." At this point Frost abandons his search. The poem has several interesting momentums, but I wish only to emphasize that here when Frost grants himself a freedom from recording naturalistic detail, he creates a supernatural scene where the obscure mechanics of the universe are presented as inharmonious with man's ordinary hopes. On this ground the god is false, yet somehow not less "real," not less powerful.

Frost surprises us by taking the same step even when he does not construct a supernatural occasion. In "Design," he sees (and I have no doubt that this poem reproduces actual experiences or at least combines several) a white spider holding a dead, white moth on an albino form of a normally blue flower. Not the gluttonous spider nor the pitiful moth, but the perversity of the flower's being white perfects the mood of metaphysical disgust in the poem. Nor does it seem to me that Frost stacks the deck. Rather, because the poem strains our credulity it forces us, perhaps paradoxically, to believe in the reality of the poem—the accident of so much whiteness could not, we feel, have been made up; it would have to have happened. And when Frost, like his reader, is caught in the paradox of believing when the circumstances are not entirely believable, the conclusion falls like a white doom:

> What had that flower to do with being white,
> The wayside blue and innocent heal-all?
> What brought the kindred spider to that height,
> Then steered the white moth thither in the night?
> What but design of darkness to appall?—
> If design govern in a thing so small.

In short, even Frost's nearest nature, even the intimate nature of "The Pasture," is able at any moment to furnish examples of an alien interference. And when Frost turns away from tangibles in Vermont, when he gazes at the far edges of the universe, he often replays the theme of the uncaring Demiurge. In "Stars" he may momentarily feel that the constellations have some kinship with man, but shortly their impersonality reveals itself:

Those stars like some snow-white
Minerva's snow-white marble eyes
Without the gift of sight.

Perhaps because he has felt such a separation between himself and the outer cosmos, Frost has tended to give up the hunt when he hears the Demiurge's laugh. No harm in that, but there is something very like harm in his tendency to veer toward an anti-intellectualism when confronted by the uncaring false god who, he fears, may after all be a true god. In that wry poem "The Star-Splitter" Brad McLaughlin burns his house down for the insurance money with which to buy a telescope. The reaction of the poet-narrator is one of amused tolerance toward such dishonesty, and though it is confessed that he and Bradford "said some of the best things we ever said" while they play with the telescope, the final question in the poem is "What good is a telescope?"

We've looked and looked, but after all where are we?

This disappointing shrug, this pragmatic reluctance, repeated in such poems as "On Looking Up by Chance at the Constellations" and varied in "The Bear," is, however, not the ultimate position. It is a step toward a final consideration; it is a moment, very possibly, of fatigue where he pauses and then steps on. In "Desert Places," for example, there remains some practical scoffing in "They cannot scare me with their empty spaces / Between stars," yet Frost makes a declarative parallel between himself and the vacant stare of space. "I have it in me so much nearer home / To scare myself with my own desert places."

But before he can go on a humble attitude must prevail, humbler than that ironic, insular practicality that smiles at Bradford McLaughlin. He must yield to the mood of separation between himself and star. It is as if he must acknowledge that sudden breaking which is a form of death. He must allow himself the bitter luxury of such a degrading acceptance of distance, separateness in the uncaring universe that his imagination, in order to survive at all, rises to a higher level. It must hold all this negation and purify it. And how very well "An Old Man's Winter Night" holds and purifies! The poem is remarkably better than "The Star-Splitter" because it is committed to the assertion of a self-limiting mood without distraction or facile didacticism. And it has remarkable interest. It begins by observing a separateness between man and a greater, outer nature:

> All out-of-doors looked darkly in at him
> Through the thin frost, almost in separate stars,
> That gathers on the pane in empty rooms.

One tarries to approve the competent observation of the frost-stars. And one may well feel that a spiritual ice is crystallizing with the frost. More importantly, however, the poem proceeds to imbue the old man with a bleakness as devastating as that found in the universe:

> What kept his eyes from giving back the gaze
> Was the lamp tilted near them in his hand.

Age, confusion, emptiness intensify in the poem until they balance the outer night. Indeed, in a poetic shift, the outer night becomes terrified of the old man. Just as impersonal nature becomes the animate observer of man, the old man becomes the impersonal—perhaps depersonified—observer of nature—his vacant peering becomes more eerily inhuman than that of the stars. In equating man's inner terror with that of the whole world the poem nods in the direction of "Desert Places," but beyond it, too, to the perception of an austere unity among all things, to the comity between man and star as in "Lost in Heaven," where the experience of heavenly disorientation becomes exultation. Even so, the goal of Frost's poetry is more than exultation. It is exaltation. There are a few steps more.

[29]

III

One perceives elements of strain and efforts at an accommodation of the outer nature from time to time. Frost would come to terms. In "A Star in a Stone-Boat" he smilingly tells of a fallen meteorite carried from where it fell to be used:

for building stone, and I, as though
Commanded in a dream, forever go
To right the wrong that this should have been so.

Yet ask where else it could have gone as well,
I do not know—I cannot stop to tell:
He might have left it lying where it fell.

From following walls I never lift my eye
Except at night to places in the sky
Where showers of charted meteors let fly.

Some may know what they seek in school and church,
And why they seek it there; for what I search
I must go measuring stone walls, perch on perch;

Sure that though not a star of death and birth,
So not to be compared, perhaps, in worth
To such resorts of life as Mars and Earth,

Though not, I say, a star of death and sin
It yet has poles, and only needs a spin
To show its worldly nature and begin

To chafe and shuffle in my calloused palm
And run off in strange tangents with my arm
As fish do with the line in first alarm.

Such as it is, it promises the prize
Of the one world complete in any size
That I am like to compass, fool or wise.

One savors the self-deprecation at the end, a self-deprecation
akin to the anti-intellectuality in "The Star-Splitter," but one
also savors the ambiguity with which the poem regards the star.
If the poem wonders whether or not it is right to use the fallen
star in building a wall, it also wonders whether or not a star
may be adopted into the family. It is, after all, a star that can
be held in the hand. There is less ambiguity in the little poem
"The Freedom of the Moon":

I put it shining anywhere I please.
By walking slowly on some evening later,
I've pulled it from a crate of crooked trees,
And brought it over glossy water, greater,
And dropped it in, and seen the image wallow,
The color run, all sorts of wonder follow.

Less ambiguity and greater presumption. One feels the presumption become sentimentality, as indeed, in an inverted way,
the humility borders on sentimentality in "Canis Major":

The great Overdog.
That heavenly beast
With a star in one eye,
Gives a leap in the east. . . .

I'm a poor underdog,
But tonight I will bark
With the great Overdog
That romps through the dark.

One does not judge these poems harshly unless he harshly
judges Frost's passionate wish to bring man and the farthest
reaches of nature together. In the last analysis Frost himself is

the victim when the old man and the stars frighten each other with the emotionless incommunication of their gaze. Let them come together! So his poem mutters in its undercurrents. And if Frost cannot quite manage a convergence of the twain, he can discover a moon (which is never so remote to farmer and astronomer alike as stars) in an attitude of love, an attitude suspiciously human. In "Moon Compasses":

> And a masked moon had spread down compass rays
> To a cone mountain in the midnight haze,
> As if the final estimate were hers,
> And as it measured in her calipers,
> The mountain stood exalted in its place.
> So love will take between the hands a face. . . .

So perhaps after all the moon can be adopted into the human family. Yet Frost hardly offers any image which brings the stars into intimate range. Even when ("Fireflies in the Garden") fireflies "emulate" the stars and "Achieve at times a very star-like start," they still cannot "sustain the part." Yet we might remember the mountain that stands "exalted in its place," and we might ask what is involved in the exaltation.

The answer may be too simple, though the effort for Frost of reaching the answer is almost too difficult. Frost tries by pulling down the heavens to elevate man. Too easy, you will say. But, of course. Yet mark how hard it has been for Frost to bring himself to do it. I have already listed some less than satisfying examples. There are others. In the first of these examples, "An Unstamped Letter in Our Rural Mail Box," the narrator is a "tramp astrologer" who sees:

> The largest firedrop ever formed
> From two stars' having coalesced
> Went streaking molten down the west.

And then this highly improbable astronomical accident is paralleled by an inner experience:

[32]

                                    Inside the brain
Two memories . . . quivered toward each other, lipped
Together, and together slipped;
And for a moment all was plain
That men have thought about in vain.

The purpose behind the parallel is clearly that of gathering
together the most unique and intimate of experiences with the
most unique and remote—in order to transform thought and
matter into meta-equivalents. The difficulty with the poem is
that it goes on too long beyond its climax and is willfully thrown
away in some stringy, overly colloquial lines. It is finally lost
altogether in a poor comic rhyme at the end. My second example suffers from similar inadequacies, but they come to us
in a different order. "Skeptic" begins in a comic-metaphysical
vein:

        Far star that tickles for me my sensitive plate
        And fries a couple of ebon atoms white.

(I have known some who were so misled by the jocularity of
this opening that they failed to see how the image drawn from
photography merges with an ocular image and deliriously im-
agined that Frost is speaking of the difficulties of wearing
dentures.) The middle section of the poem, after the misplaced
cleverness of the opening, asserts in a breathy, naïve voice that
Frost does not believe that this nova is the last star nor even
that it is "after explosion going away so fast." So far the reader
is apt to squirm, but in the last section a startling transfusion—
an osmosis—between stars and the human sensibility takes
place:

    The universe may or may not be very immense.
    As a matter of fact there are times when I am apt
    To feel it close in tight against my sense
    Like a caul in which I was born and still am wrapped.

[33]

The last two lines are among Frost's finest and ought not to have been wasted in an organically impossible and freakish poem. Yet, taking the lines by themselves, they quite majestically and honestly draw together the intimate nature of self and the separate nature of the universe. They achieve this collusion without the mutual terror of old man and cosmos in "An Old Man's Winter Night." And in these lines we glimpse a finished gesture where faith, brought to bay, extends the human mind and heart to the margins of a disappearing God. Heart and mind remain as human as Job.

In effect, then, the desire (and the power) to assemble inner and outer nature in a given poem is essentially Frost's desire to discover balance, or, failing discovery, to *achieve* it. Even in the cozy, nearby landscape of farm and woods, Frost pushes in one direction, one extreme, then backtracks and moves in another direction. He may feel an entire identification or communion in "Hyla Brook," but in another poem, such as "Range-Finding," he may stand aside distressed and removed, refusing yet contemplating the rather Melvillean vision of the grinding necessities of instinct in nature. Because he brings the naturalist's loyalty to truth to his observation of nature he cannot ignore the blunt facts. However, he can bring nature's instinctual, trancelike sprawl ultimately into line with man's conscious idealism, as he does in "Two Look at Two." Here a man and woman see a doe and a buck and are in turn inspected by them. The animals remain animals, the human beings remain human. The two discrete worlds nevertheless momentarily fuse, or at least the wall between them becomes transparent:

> Two had seen two, whichever side you spoke from.
> 'This *must* be all.' It was all. Still they stood,
> A great wave from it going over them,
> As if the earth in one unlooked-for favor
> Had made them certain earth returned their love.

In Frost's poems, then, a pattern emerges. At the level of intimate nature, Frost perceives the heart-warming yet too

[34]

facile relationships between himself and the superficial aspects of nature. Or, he perceives a frightening severance between himself and the colossal drift of nature. Ultimately, some poems emerge (such as "Two Look at Two") in which he brings the extreme views into equilibrium. At the level of outer nature, he feels inevitable the separation between man and the circling stars. Yet he can, though the effort is exhausting, bring these two worlds together. And in both cases love or faith seems to be the catalyst which while not entering into the combination nevertheless brings it about. Such poems either belong with or preordain Frost's masterpieces. All else is experiment, a walking back and forth on the earth. But a necessary experiment, a necessary perambulation.

THREE

The Poet as Naturalist

I

As the naturalist who is trustful of his senses, Frost has had
to experience with the poet's burning irritability what is un-
doubtedly the most basic distress of modern life. Not war, for
that is not a peculiarly modern problem. He has had to observe
modern man's awesome effort to escape nature. At the same
time he has had to observe that the very science which sponsors
such an escape is based on laws that suggest no escape is possible. Man has risen to extranatural levels because his science
has gazed at the casual drift of nature, has discovered laws and
used them as a bird uses the wind to fly against the wind. Yet
these laws seem inexorable and equally seem to demand the
ultimate death of all things. So that murmuring below the surface of the modern consciousness is the question as to whether
man, because he is aware of natural law and to a degree able
to use it, can by that knowledge prove himself superior to the
law. Or whether he himself must follow the law which im-
partially condemns the passenger pigeon, brontosaurus, or nova.
The staunchest Tennysonian among us must ask if he should not
follow the glum rather than the gleam.

It would be wrong to call such an uncertainty dilemma, for
nothing about it seems within the will power or choice of man
to change or effect. The young Charles Darwin wondered where
the evidence of his collecting and cataloguing would take him;
with the self-sacrifice of a religious martyr he allowed it to take
him where it had to. Not that he wanted to go there. It is a
pleasant coincidence that Frost has expressed his admiration of

Darwin's journal of his first youthful expedition aboard the "Beagle." Half seriously, one may suggest that Darwin's juvenile book is like a long poem by Frost. True, it begins less in delight than in seasickness, and it ends less in wisdom than in an approach to knowledge, a half-realized formulation. Still, it proceeds joyfully with one observation after another, as if the generalization to come would also be joyous, as if the understanding of the experience would be as rapturous as the experience itself had been. Or better, as if generalization and understanding could somehow be ignored. But the price of looking without sentimentality at nature is knowledge of decay, death, and of the cold teeth beneath nature's lips. Mark Twain and Herman Melville felt this truth in Darwin's century. And the twentieth century has confirmed rather than denied these despairing intuitions—even despite the ambivalent cosmogonies of contemporary physics. Indeed, this is the century which has taken to measuring the epochs of time by decay, the slow death of radioactive carbon, and it is in the twentieth century that Frost, at heart a naturalist in the sense that he is incapable of ceasing to observe, writes.

It is not, of course, that the problem of the twentieth century is much different, really, from that of any other. Only that it is intensified by a preponderance of evidence and learning. Poets in any age or any civilization have brooded over the circumstances in Frost's "In Hardwood Groves":

> Before the leaves can mount again
> To fill the trees with another shade,
> They must go down past things coming up.
> They must go down into the dark decayed.
>
> They *must* be pierced by flowers and put
> Beneath the heel of dancing flowers.
> However it is in some other world
> I know that this is the way in ours.

[37]

The poem may not be Frost's most memorable, but it beauti-fully asserts one of the primary attitudes underlying Frost's poetry. Change is the presumed necessity of nature—though Frost often camouflages the attitude, as soldiers camouflage themselves with green branches. Once again, to be sure, poets have always paused, awed by the repetitive drama of nature; they have prodded it, as if they hoped after all to find some-thing happy in the sullen pattern. The theme, indeed, is one by which to measure a poet. Lucretius could content himself with the surety that only change is permanent. Spenser could allow the power of mutability and yet rescue man from its toils through Christian humanism. Shelley catalogued the cycle of nature partly for its inherent grandeur but also because he saw it as prelude to a more thrilling drama, the will's triumph over even the decrees of fate. But these are the relatively simple reactions, Epicurean, renaissance, romantic. Frost's is not quite any of these though it partakes of all.

Despite one serious technical lapse, a better and more il-luminating poem than "In Hardwood Groves" is "The Wood-Pile":

> It was a cord of maple, cut and split
> And piled—and measured, four by four by eight....
> No runner tracks in this year's snow looped near it.
> And it was older sure than this year's cutting,
> Or even last year's or the year's before.
> The wood was gray and the bark warping off it
> And the pile somewhat sunken. Clematis
> Had wound strings round and round it like a bundle.
> What held it though on one side was a tree
> Still growing, and on one a stake and prop,
> These latter about to fall. I thought that only
> Someone who lived in turning to fresh tasks
> Could so forget his handiwork on which
> He spent himself, the labor of his ax,

And leave it there far from a useful fireplace
To warm the frozen swamp as best it could
With the slow smokeless burning of decay.

Here, the notion of nature's eternal rotation is barely suggested, even though it anchors the poem. Even so, I read "the slow smokeless burning of decay" and I am humbled before the sheer massiveness of time; I am linked in the chain of the world's births and deaths. Still, this is not all, nor is it the reason for the effectiveness of the phrase. The encyclical has been redirected by the poem through a near paradox. The "smokeless burning of decay" is assigned the purpose of warming a frozen swamp. In other words, though the woodpile is literally unused and deserted, it is, in a larger vision performing a task. Though the woodpile is decaying, the decay nevertheless in the whole patient momentum of nature is a conflagration. But is not the notion of warming a swamp ironical? Does it not merely emphasize human loss and bleakness? It does have such an emphasis, catching us into hopeless grief, but it seems also to impose a curious purposiveness or even a human intention—not a pathetic fallacy but a pathetic rectitude—on nature. For a moment the phrase makes a glassy fusion of human spirit and the rigors of chemistry, as if they both sought the same thing and both were blind as to what that thing is.

II

Just so: Because the wishes, the yearnings of humanity will not be silenced it is impossible to treat Frost's view of the oscillations of nature in any abstract way. For Frost is continuously up to his old trick of using his own view—as indeed anything that comes to hand—as a basis for comparing and contrasting, evaluating humankind. This being so, we are hardly astounded to find him falling occasionally into the bitterest attitude. It is an attitude, however, which if comprehensible is illogical. It runs something like this: The grand pattern of decline and renewal, birth and death, summer and winter comes to represent an eternity or permanence. Well, this has a Heraclitean truth, for the pattern seems to go on forever, yet pragmatically the pattern is made up of death as well as rebirth. It does represent a great tidal continuum, yet within it there is no true continuity of time or consciousness nor of body. There is, then, no true rebirth but only a large symbol of rebirth. In Frost's mind there exists a corollary to the attitude. This pattern of birth and decay in nature, once established as a permanent recurrence, is contrasted with decay itself in such a way as to imbue with greater poignancy the transience of phenomena—including man.

The attitude is not limited to any particular school or century (illogicality never has been), though perhaps as the reverse of the romantic question "If winter comes can spring be far behind?" one finds it most intensely explored in the romantic mind. Frost, however, does not pursue the quarry very far. And indeed he treats the attitude almost purely as mood, eluding argument, as in the little lyric "Nothing Gold Can Stay" or in the more ambitious "The Oven Bird":

> There is a singer everyone has heard
>
> . . . .
>
> He says that leaves are old and that for flowers
> Mid-summer is to spring as one to ten.
>
> . . . .
>
> He says the highway dust is over all.
> The bird would cease and be as other birds
> But that he knows in singing not to sing.
> The question that he frames in all but words
> Is what to make of a diminished thing.

What indeed to make of a diminished thing? One can backtrack, reverse the equation, as Frost certainly does in "The Onset," where he observes:

the snow may heap
In long storms an undrifted four feet deep
As measured against maple, birch, and oak,
It cannot check the peeper's silver croak;
And I shall see the snow all go down hill
In water of a slender April rill . . .

The mood is real and pleasant, but one does have the right to
suggest that if summer comes, then winter will be right along.
Admittedly, the suggestion demands that emotion be tested by
reason, and I should not trouble with the obvious except that
Frost himself seems troubled.

Let us reconsider this problem which almost inevitably stares
wryly in the face of the naturalist. All nature changes continuously. Any discrete part of the change—a man, a flower, a
season—is transient, but the rhythmic total picture of change
may be viewed as an abstract permanence. A permanence, then,
composed of impermanences. So far, understandable, though
not quite satisfyingly rational. However, add an ingredient. I
call the ingredient "an emotional rejection of transience." One
is almost ashamed to call it anything, for there is nothing unusual in the rejection. All to some degree share it. Yet surely
for the person whose senses are always trained to the sequences
of nature, such a rejection is particularly poignant. For Frost it
is the divine troublemaker. A philosopher would ultimately
have to take one side or the other. The poet can play the whole
contradiction as that kind of truth which, if not absolute, is at
least true to human experience. A case, then, perhaps for fallibility as an approach to poetry.

Make no mistake about it. Though Frost would prefer to
temporize, shore up the ruins, when run down and brought to
bay he will make the honest confession of fallibility. He is
brought to bay in the poem "The Times Table." The bitter
farmer may say to his mare:

A sigh for every so many a breath,

[41]

And for every so many sigh a death.
That's what I always tell my wife
Is the multiplication table of life.

But the statement is too resolute for Frost. He adds:

The saying may be ever so true;
But it's just the kind of a thing that you
Nor I, nor nobody else may say,
Unless our purpose is doing harm,
And then I know of no better way
To close a road, abandon a farm,
Reduce the births of the human race,
And bring back nature in people's place.

One should in this poem be less aware of the slovenly logic than of the effort to fly in the face of logic. Death is the cadence of life, and yet it is wrong to say so. To say so brings "back nature in people's place." This ought not to be such an ill fate to one who more often than not admires nature. But it is. So ill a fate that Frost will listen to the farmer's words, allow them to be true, and yet reject them as somehow wrong. True but wrong, then.

It is only fair, however, to admit that Frost is capable of another mood, as in the poem "Our Hold on the Planet," in which he argues that unless "nature altogether . . . including human nature" were "a fraction of one percent" on the side of man, "our hold on the planet wouldn't have so increased." This view, based not on "nature altogether," but on a short, unscientific view, cannot but seem suspicious and sentimental. The sovereign attitude, sadder, more real, and clearer-eyed, is an extension of the true-but-wrong mood. It characterizes his reactions to outer space or to the work-a-day census taker who must record the decline of New England towns:

The melancholy of having to count souls
Where they grow fewer and fewer every year

Is extreme where they shrink to none at all.
It must be I want life to go on living.

The desire for "life to go on living," rather than the certainty
that it will, has saved Frost from the ardent despair of the
twentieth century. And Frost deliberately has set about making
his view public and unequivocal. At times he speaks of the bad
sages, the doomists, the deceiving poets. In his poetic drama
A Masque of Mercy Robinson Jeffers and Eugene O'Neill are
referred to with humorous tolerance as "dungeoneers" and
"stokers" in the make-believe hell beneath the bookstore. In his
latest volume, *In the Clearing* (1962), a poem with the comic
title "Our Doom to Bloom" alludes to Jeffers' poem "Shine,
Perishing Republic." And I am told that once as he boarded a
Boston-bound train to keep a luncheon engagement with T. S.
Eliot he remarked that he had a rendezvous with death.

Presumably, Frost accepts the vision of doom and simultaneously rejects it, either as a harmful way of thinking or as an easy
surrender to romantic excess. He himself knows the temptation
of the easy surrender and speaks of it in "On the Heart's Beginning to Cloud the Mind." From a train window he sees in
bleak desert country a light in a house—one light "maintained
against the night . . . with a God-forsaken brute despair." Then
Frost shifts ground, deciding after all that "Life is not so
sinister-grave." He has deluded himself or been deluded by the
setting. This poem is curiously self-defeating, however. We
are given a convincing scene which creates a dark mood. Then
all is cast aside for a "sensible" view. One cannot deny that the
poem may be experientially true, but still the poem prepares
the mind for being clouded by the heart—not at all for the
mind's suddenly clarifying everything. To assess the divisive
character of the poem one needs only to contrast it with the
undiverted and mounting pressure of "Once by the Pacific,"
comparing, for example, the declination of "matter of fact has
made them brave" in "On the Heart's Beginning to Cloud the
Mind" with the sudden bold pressure of

[43]

> There would be more than ocean-water broken
> Before God's last *Put out the Light* was spoken.

But "On the Heart's Beginning to Cloud the Mind" is a disappointing poem only partly for the reason that it brings in a conclusion at odds with the atmosphere. More deeply, by trying to elude the sentimentality of the impressionable heart, it inadvertently sentimentalizes the mind. Its very common sense becomes a violation of the possibilities of the poem—almost a vulgar intrusion, certainly an exaggeration.

To be sure, a common sense view, properly incorporated, is not unfriendly to poetry, and Frost has incorporated it properly on many occasions. The crisp, reserved poem "Neither out far nor in Deep" offers an example. The poem avoids distance and depth, merely glancing without editorial at the simplest phenomena, so that we may accept the level conclusion which tells us of "the people" who "look at the sea":

> They cannot look out far.
> They cannot look in deep.
> But when was that ever a bar
> To any watch they keep?

"On the Heart's Beginning to Cloud the Mind" is a little like a school composition which promises sublime terror and then finishes with, "And then I woke up." "Neither out far nor in Deep" solemnly questions man's competence, his whole future, while still admiring the abstract effort, the moderation as well as the courage. Not even this attempt takes the reader to the moment of acquiescence. It is not enough to accept; we must run with the poem. Frost has tried two other strategies.

The first strategy seems to be that of reversing his field altogether—a whistling in the dark, sheer bravado. From "Riders":

> What is this talked-of mystery of birth
> But being mounted bareback on the earth?
> We can just see the infant up astride,
> His small fist buried in the bushy hide.

> There is our wildest mount—a headless horse.
> But though it runs unbridled off its course,
> And all our blandishments would seem defied,
> We have ideas yet that we haven't tried.

If the bravado is almost too much, at least in the half-sensuous, half-frantic image of the infant mounted on the massive horse, the spirit of the poem is given incarnation. And certainly it is not hard to sympathize with Frost's wish to combat the tiresome reiteration of despair. One does find an increasing tendency through his career toward a guarded optimism, as though he had deliberately set about arguing the case with his contemporaries:

> There may be little or much beyond the grave,
> But the strong are saying nothing until they see.

So Frost says, and says quite honestly. And perhaps any of these efforts would seem enough, and we should be content with their heartiness, if it were not for the fact that he has managed his case upon more than one occasion as the master poet, a true legislator. And he has managed without reversing his naturalist's instinct, without compromise and without Browning's bravado. The second strategy then.

In a relatively early poem "The Exposed Nest" Frost tells about finding a nest of newly hatched birds exposed by the cutter bar "to the heat and light." There is a question as to whether to shade the birds with grass, for to do so would perhaps keep the mother from returning. "We saw the risk we took in doing good." Yet they do it "to prove we cared." The poem finishes:

> Why is there then
> No more to tell? We turned to other things.
> I haven't any memory—have you?—
> Of ever coming to the place again
> To see if the birds lived the first night through,
> And so at last to learn to use their wings.

[45   ]

The ending is cruel but morally honest, and the laconic "We turned to other things" is preparation for one of Frost's most successful poems "Out, Out—." The dramatic situation of this poem is simple. A boy, "doing a man's work," loses his hand in a buzz saw, "sees all spoiled."

> The doctor put him in the dark of ether.
> He lay and puffed his lips out with his breath.
> And then—the watcher at his pulse took fright.
> No one believed. They listened at his heart.
> Little—less—nothing!—and that ended it.
> No more to build on there. And they, since they
> Were not the one dead, turned to their affairs.

We must ask what happens at the most basic level in these poems. One sees life, bird or boy, menaced by faceless accident, nobody's fault. Simultaneously, one sees the human watchers touched by normal griefs and fears. And yet life must turn to a more important task finally, that of continuing. Essentially, then, Frost makes life capable of surviving by purifying it, by reducing its sentiment and maximizing its resolve, all of which is a different thing from saying "but perhaps we don't know" or of whooping it up about the capabilities of the human spirit to ride anything. Life triumphs here because it is seen as the great duty. Life triumphs by being as stubborn as nature, not more so. In these poems Frost speaks from the very depths of his personality. Such expression is painful, of course, and one is not surprised that it has only rarely come. But whether rare or common is of little matter. What matters is that only the grand composer could hold together in one poem the two severe and mutually accusing ideas that one must be moved to pity and compassion and that one must coldly and sternly pursue the duty of endurance and survival. And if Frost has never again explored this theme with such deadly directness as in "Out, Out—," still in the late poem "The Lesson for Today" his pen moves with a flourish over the theme, as if he knew that he had said all that he could years before, and he now dreamily covers the bleak clay with a charming and civilizing glaze:

> We all are doomed to broken-off careers,
> And so's the nation, so's the total race.
> The earth itself is liable to the fate
> Of meaninglessly being broken off.
> (And hence so many literary tears
> At which my inclination is to scoff.)
> I may have wept that any should have died
> Or missed their chance, or not have been their best,
> Or been their riches, fame, or love denied;
> On me as much as any is the jest.
> I take my incompleteness with the rest.
> God bless himself can no one else be blessed.
>
> I hold your doctrine of Memento Mori.
> And were an epitaph to be my story
> I'd have a short one ready for my own.
> I would have written of me on my stone:
> I had a lover's quarrel with the world.

FOUR

Heaven and Earth

I

This chapter is concerned with the root and branch of two recurrent motives in Robert Frost's poetry. The second of these, the aspiration toward some kind of heaven is the more important, but one comes to it through the first, which involves a "withdrawal into wilderness." At the risk of tedium one must ponder once again what must be all the possible effects, all the extremities of sensibility which accrue to the poet who is a naturalist. The senses and the mind are trained upon whatever is there to be perceived. This is his primary source of understanding. Yet let us suppose that the mind does not like what the senses convey, or can find no meaning in it. In such cases there must follow either a disenchantment or a repugnance between mind and the senses. Another way of putting all this is to say that aspiration or intuition may fortify the mind against the bare limits of induction. The aspiring intuition may be drawn toward a mystic-religious belief quite counter to nature; or if not counter, greater in the sense that it includes and supersedes nature. It may be drawn toward a rationalistic concept seemingly at least more personally and humanly desirable than the helical rhythms of the natural world. My assumption is that just as Frost strives for a synthesis between an intimate and remote nature and between a transient and permanent nature, so here, too, where nature and the spirit seem at odds, strain develops, and he would like to resolve the matter. He would like to know how far one may dare trust nature, and how far one may dare trust intuition. But he would like to trust both.

The burden of such strain appears early in Frost's poetry in that curious poem "The Demiurge's Laugh," which, we remember, begins "It was far in the sameness of the wood." *The sameness of the wood:* Associations crowd the phrase, but primarily and without difficulty, the reader can feel in "sameness," an impression of having lost one's way. That moment in the woods when all things look alike, landmarks are lost, direction fails. Now, it may be profitably remembered that "The Demiurge's Laugh" is a poem which conceives nature as a Siva-like destroyer and creator, and that Frost in this poem is trying to track "the demon" down even though he knows what he hunts is "no true god." In other words Frost implies that there is a point at which observation of nature becomes a meaningless maze and ceases to yield evidence. To say so, however, is to convert the phrase "sameness of the wood" into a symbolic equivalent of being lost in the search for truth.

In a poem from the same (first) book, "A Dream Pang," Frost makes an arrangement similar, though simpler, to the one in "The Demiurge's Laugh."

> I had withdrawn in forest, and my song
> Was swallowed up in leaves that blew away . . .

The lines suggest that in being lost in nature Frost feels a loss of self, or at least some challenge to the self. However, the moment when bearings disappear is often also a fructifying moment. In "The Wood-Pile," before the poem moves toward its miraculous conclusion, Frost is lost in "sameness":

> The view was all in lines
> Straight up and down of tall slim trees
> Too much alike to mark or name a place by
> So as to say for certain I was here
> Or somewhere else: I was just far from home.

Sometimes an atmosphere of physiological (though surely psychological) irritation marks the moment:

It's when I'm weary of considerations,
And life is too much like a pathless wood
Where your face burns and tickles with the cobwebs
Broken across it, and one eye is weeping
From a twig's having lashed across it open.

Here in "Birches," of course, the sequel is not exactly the same, for there is less a fructifying moment of discovery than a retreat from "considerations." And yet it is a psychologically comprehensible extension of the same strain. For if nature observed, like a word repeated over and over, suddenly loses all meaning, a moment of terrified confusion breaks upon the naturalist. In this moment he may be incapable of awaiting discovery. He may only wish to escape the moment. And whither may he escape, this captive of nature? Obviously, if earth is to be abandoned, heaven remains. In some such interplay of thought and feeling, nature destroys itself for Frost. In the sameness of the wood design is lost, chaos returns to the face of the deep, and he must either penetrate the chaos or yearn for paradise. The yearning is repeated again and again, finding its appropriate symbolization in the poetry.

Surely, it is by reason of this tension, this urgency that Robert Frost calls his latest book *In the Clearing*. True, he has publicly related the title to the poem "The Pasture," in which the poet would watch the water clear in the newly cleaned spring. Yet surely the title has more than one meaning. Surely the poem "A Cabin in the Clearing" profoundly reflects the title. For here it is: a solution of a kind wherein the aspirant human condition is surrounded by the opacity of the woods but within its mortal boundaries is nevertheless separated from them. Even so the ending of "A Cabin in the Clearing" continues something of the ambiguity of earlier poems. If the clearing contains the human need to comprehend, the woods remain as inscrutable as ever. Indeed, the prognosis is hardly certain:

Than smoke and mist who better could appraise
The kindred spirit of an inner haze.

[50]

II

For Frost the schism between earth and heaven is mirrored in a pair of conformations which parallel each other and transcend the schism. These conformations are central to an appreciation of the poetry, for they are absolutely central to Frost. All of his important poems move one way or another from a plexus where a discontent with the book of nature tempts him toward a celestial journey. Nor does the story end with temptation.

If on the one hand Frost can write a poem ("On the Heart's Beginning to Cloud the Mind") about mental responsibility versus emotional perception, he can, on the other hand and quite as readily, write a poem on the same theme with an exactly opposite conclusion. Now, it may be here, as Sidney Cox has suggested, that Frost refuses to make up his mind or to take a final stand, but I do not honestly believe so. I think Frost is an exploratory poet, inching in upon his commitment from many sides, along many oblique paths, so that many of his poems are way stations rather than final statements—gradients rather than the full measures of his opinion and insight. I have heard Frost say that his poems capture a feeling of "sometimes it seems as if." I take this to mean that he does not necessarily hold them out as ultimate utterances—many of them can represent only the limited and fallible apperception, the step rather than the journey. Herman Melville, it will be recalled, complained in a letter that it was unfair to hold a poet answerable forever for what was true for him only in the moment. And so, if the heart seems at times to cloud the mind, it is not necessarily a contradiction in Frost that the mind may at another time be accused of dragging down the heart. At this point it is desirable to introduce the first of the transcending parallels to the dilemma of the malcontent naturalist.

In "Too Anxious for Rivers" Frost observes:

> What set us on fire and what set us revolving
> Lucretius the Epicurean might tell us

'Twas something we knew all about to begin with
And needn't have fared into space like his master
To find 'twas the effort, the essay of love.

The poem verges on what I consider the least engaging aspect of Frost's poetry, a tendency toward anti-intellectualism. But it only verges, for it seems written in some kind of private conversation or in a blurred allegory wherein the substitution of terms seems more important than the actual words and perhaps even more important than the eventual meaning. Science represents the kind of knowledge that the naturalist-observer possesses—and the limit of that knowledge. Love represents a different but unlimited step toward wisdom. As I put it, it sounds mildly Platonic, but I think that is more the result of our having always to gasp, stutter, and make vague sounds when we try to express that kind of understanding which is other than mathematical or immediately evident to the senses.

More to the point, we may see here that the evidence of the senses, science, seems a clumsy, even tedious method of searching for truth, while love is linked with intuitive discovery (as against proven discovery). Thus, Lucretius' *De Rerum Natura* begins with a hymn to Venus. I think we may further see why a person like Frost whose practice both as poet and thinker is evidential or scientific can turn at times such anti-intellectual scorn upon science, calling it impractical, nosy, or foolish. It is a simple matter of impatience. But one must be prepared to believe that despite impatience Frost is never quite willing to abandon the scientific view. Indeed, rather than that, he would prefer to transmute it into a religion or (marvel of irony) into a superstition. Hence one need not be amazed to discover that upon occasion Frost may treat a scientific theory with the tenderness usually accorded myth. For example, he speaks of the beginning of life in these terms:

And if men have watched a long time
And never seen sun-smitten slime

Again come to life and crawl off,
We must not be too ready to scoff.

Though this particular theory is contrary to the cherished notion
of special creation, though it quarrels absolutely with religion,
Frost's tone is that of a protector of the faith. The poem
("Sitting By a Bush in Broad Sunlight") finishes:

God once spoke to people by name.
The sun once imparted its flame.
One impulse persists as our breath;
The other persists as our faith.

Not only does science receive a religious defense, but the theory
is supported by religious myth (in the title's reference to the
burning bush) and by intuition, as we see by the final de-
pendency on "faith." To a degree the poem makes a quaint
synthesis of science and religion. The more usual position for
Frost is to translate science and religion into the terms "love"
and "thought" and then to work toward a synthesis of these
substituted terms, though permitting them at times to remain
discrete and quarrelsome. "Love," he tells us, "has earth to
which she clings" while "Thought has a pair of dauntless
wings" ("Bond and Free"). Nevertheless, he concludes:

Thought cleaves the interstellar gloom
And sits in Sirius' disc all night,
Till day makes him retrace his flight,
With smell of burning on every plume,
Back past the sun to an earthly room.

His gains in heaven are what they are.
Yet some say Love by being thrall
And simply staying possesses all
In several beauty that Thought fares far
To find fused in another star.

I take it that Love or intuition or perhaps humble observation may come to the same conclusion as austere thought or science. In this poem Frost can make no choice between love and thought though the reader may feel that love is the sweetest way of finding the elegant secrets of the universe.

The same desire for syntheses as well as a similar dubiety about gaining them informs the second transcending conformation, where Frost's translation becomes blunt and where the poems graduate toward a more impressive profundity: where the opposed terms become simply "heaven" and "earth." A qualification, however. The heaven-earth poems are not necessarily profound, though they have a better chance of being so. It is helpful to begin with a rather arch little poem "Fragmentary Blue." Why make so much of a blue bird or blue butterfly, Frost asks. He answers that:

> Since earth is earth, perhaps, not heaven (as yet)—
> Though some savants make earth include the sky;
> And blue so far above us comes so high
> It only gives our wish for blue a whet.

If the poem were not such a trifler it would seem false. The relations are mechanical equivalents rather than imaginative ones. Nevertheless the desire to interchange heaven and earth is very clear. Perhaps one feels that the desire is so intensified that it obscures Frost's good taste and encourages him to treat as a little joke one of his deepest themes. But we can go on to more important expressions.

In a later poem "A Steeple on the House" Frost says that "A spire and belfry coming on the roof / Means that a soul is coming on the flesh." And with this statement we are face to face with the symbol which virtually stalks Frost's poems, a symbol oddly enough linked with his symbol of being lost in the woods. It stands with no uncertainty for the urge toward heaven. As we ordinarily encounter the symbol, it is a guileless one—a ladder, a tree, some perpendicular, then, geometric in clarity and simplicity, yet organic always within the poem itself.

Three important poems come to mind, "Birches," "Wild Grapes" and "After Apple-Picking."

Behind the poem "Birches," which now seems a public domain, behind the humor, the grace as well as the endearing flaws, stands Frost's need to choose between heaven's truth and earth's truth, between deductive and inductive knowledge of the universe. The need is apparent as well as his inability—finally —to choose at all. He begins in "Birches" by setting forth "fact." But even as he does so he begins to destroy the fact, fracturing it in prisms of imagery, cartooning as Shelley did in "The Cloud" and "The Sensitive Plant" or as fantastic children love to do, until he arrives at one of the most absurd comparisons in all poetry:

> You may see their trunks arching in the woods
> Years afterwards, trailing their leaves on the ground
> Like girls on hands and knees that throw their hair
> Before them over their heads to dry in the sun.

It is best not to think of all these girls crouching in the woods. Why does Frost admit the image? Outside the question of appropriateness, the image has the effect of destroying that very "Truth . . . With all her matter-of-fact about the ice-storm." So that, told in a relatively factual tone, his "untrue" fantasy about a boy's bending the trees seems by contrast "truer." Ultimately, however, we must see the tree as an approach to heaven, and when we do, we also see that this approach is surrounded by suspense and even a species of terror. The boy, we are told,

> always kept his poise
> To the top branches, climbing carefully
> With the same pains you use to fill a cup
> Up to the brim, *and even above the brim*, [my italics]
> Then he flung outward, feet first, with a swish,
> Kicking his way down through the air to the ground.

[55]

In the end Jacob's ladder returns the boy to "earth which is the right place for love." The word "love," we may see, speaks as it does in "Too Anxious for Rivers" ("The effort, the essay of love") and in "Bond and Free" in behalf of a stay-at-home loyalty which bends the heavenward trajectory back to earth, back to the dear riot of fact. A question rises. Why bother with soaring toward heaven if one can get divine answers down on the farm? Well, because the answers seem to come *after,* not *before,* soaring toward heaven. Indeed, earth may offer only the confusion symbolized in the lost-in-the-woods figure, when he is "weary of considerations." Hence if I am correct about his symbology Frost appears to say that he becomes exasperated with seeking truth on earth through earthly means and would like to see what heaven has to say, yet he wants to go only as far toward heaven as his loyalty to life will permit. Presumably, the half-way yielding to this delicious and dangerous temptation brings illumination or at least a certainty. At any rate he does not want to buy freedom or knowledge at the cost of death. He dallies with heavenly wisdom and then returns to earth to discover through "love" which has itself been polished and sharpened in the heavenly temptation. Regarded with leniency this teeter-totter of thought and feeling suggests a desire to bring divine understanding to earth. Less leniently regarded it seems a contradictory jumble. But the truth may involve neither vague idealism nor illogicality, but a decision to divide his bets until he is sure of winning.

Written from the same matrix as "Birches," "Wild Grapes" ought to be recognized as the better poem. That is not to say that it could ever be as popular, but it has a stronger unity and, while using the same scenery as "Birches" reaches a truer, less confused conclusion. True, the poem repeats the grotesque simile between girl and birch:

> Wearing a thin head-dress of pointed leaves,
> And heavy on her heavy hair behind,
> Against her neck, an ornament of grapes.

But along with the rest of the fantasy in the poem we are ready to accept the image because it emerges from a dramatic action between two playful characters. More importantly, the poem establishes certain rights to whimsicality in that it is narrated by a woman who is ironically sportive and charmingly erudite. She alludes not merely to the Orpheus myth but also to "Leif the Lucky's German," which means that of variant saga accounts of the discovery of Vinland she has read the most obscure. And, also, if that birch-girl image does reappear, there are other images that are stunning, more valid than any in "Birches," for example, "My small wrists stretching till they showed the banjo strings." Furthermore, the poem strikes me as the more satisfying because it does not become quite so cluttered by the "considerations" and remains primarily a small but realistic victory of life over death. The mind is tempted and tempts, but the heart (the "love") triumphs:

> I had not taken the first step in knowledge;
> I had not learned to let go with the hands,
> As still I have not learned to with the heart,
> And have no wish to with the heart—nor need,
> That I can see. The mind—is not the heart.
> I may yet live, as I know others live,
> To wish in vain to let go with the mind—
> Of cares, at night, to sleep; but nothing tells me
> That I need learn to let go with the heart.

A better poem than either of these, "After Apple-Picking," ponders a harvest which has come to perfection and then gone beyond perfection. "I am over tired / Of the great harvest I myself desired." Robert Penn Warren believes that the harvest means the job of writing poetry (as Allen Tate seems to believe about the climbing motif in "Birches"). Though most good poems have symbolic extensions, halos, I feel rather stubbornly that this poem loses brilliance the moment the reader tries to make it other than a literal harvest or even other than an apple harvest. In any case the impressions of harvest are linked to both the earth-love feelings and the divine temptation which is frankly introduced in the first line of the poem: "My long two-pointed ladder's sticking through a tree / Toward heaven still." And then the harvest, just as the withdrawal into a forest destroys the definition of things for Frost, begins to lose reality. Beautifully the disintegration takes place in the mind which had sought absolute satisfaction in the earth alone:

> I am drowsing off.
> I cannot rub the strangeness from my sight
> I got from looking through a pane of glass
> I skimmed this morning from the drinking trough
> And held against the world of hoary grass.
> It melted, and I let it fall and break.
> But I was well
> Upon my way to sleep before it fell,
> And I could tell
> What form my dreaming was about to take.
> Magnified apples appear and disappear,
> Stem end and blossom end,
> And every fleck of russet showing clear.
> My instep arch not only keeps the ache,
> It keeps the pressure of a ladder round.
> I feel the ladder sway as the boughs bend.
> And I keep hearing from the cellar bin
> The rumbling sound
> Of load on load of apples coming in.

Then the woodchuck is cast—almost violently—into the final determination of the poem:

> The woodchuck could say whether it's like his
> Long sleep, as I describe its coming on,
> Or just some human sleep.

The woodchuck's hibernation is obviously a longer, hence profounder sleep. Therefore the ultimate attitude of the poem is a daring of death or a daring to let go of life after the exhausting and not absolutely satisfying experience of holding the earth in love. But it needs to be added that even here Frost speaks not of death but of sleep, of a long discontinuity, perhaps, but not of any permanent goodbye. That is why I earlier stated that I felt that in "Birches" Frost was cautiously dividing his bets. I do not mean that unless poems dedicate themselves to death they are weak! I do not mean that Frost's poems are craven or bland. But I cannot avoid the feeling that Frost, though he comes to the threshold of a final vision, willfully draws back.

When he counts the things of this world, the counting becomes a dismal repetition before which the mind reels and he finds himself in the sameness of the wood. The things, the data, the reality of nature, then, while conceived as precious and never to be abandoned, do not deliver truth to him but illusion, the sameness of the wood, the mocking, revenant apples. The things of nature bring him to irritation, which tempts him to climb a tree, a ladder toward heaven; or to exhaustion, which tempts him to contemplate a deeper than ordinary human sleep. In rejecting, however, the complete journey to heaven or the perfect sleep, he can only go back, of course, to considerations, back to harvests. But to say so is to speak rather unfairly. Frost, by his withdrawal from withdrawal casts his lot with most human beings. And it seems unlikely that most human beings will hold it against him that he will not take the step toward a final clarification of his vision. Nor will they grieve that he does not always go as far as he could. For sometimes he does.

FIVE

The Literate Farmer

If in his private soul Frost has played naturalism against intuition, in his view of the public soul, society itself, he has—though with a different success—brought similar oppositions into play. But these oppositions in the public soul, being less of the temperament than of the conscience, are somehow plainer, the patterns are simpler and the achievement more open to attack.

The poems concerned with man and nature have often led to the view that Frost is a skeptic—or, accompanied by the supercilious smile above the lectern, to the suggestion that he is not so comfy and happy after all. There is every reason to agree that there is stress, but the term *skeptic* is not quite right. Certainly, one finds skeptical poems but one finds others which by and large oppose skepticism. Are we to say that such poems neutralize each other or that they show that Frost lacks a consistent core? I am not especially cheerful about my own consistency, but my judgment here as elsewhere is that Frost makes tentative statements, trying to work through the moment into timelessness and that for him there are many moments worth contemplating, probing. He probes various possibilities before he ever reaches a thesis.

Among the poems of his first book, and among his best poems, "The Vantage Point" is instructive. In the first stanza he ponders mankind, a mankind isolated from nature, and in the second, nature separated from mankind. The only evaluation that the poem makes derives from the sense of climax that comes in speaking of inhuman nature last and in the greater attraction of the images in the second stanza. If tired of men, he has "but to turn on my arm, and lo,"

> The sun-burned hillside sets my face aglow,
> My breathing shakes the bluet like a breeze,
> I smell the earth, I smell the bruisèd plant,
> I look into the crater of the ant.

In their distortions of scale, these lines are among Frost's most compelling and imaginative, yet they do not for all their strength necessarily assert a preference for nature over man. Agreed, their power may be based upon a preference, but it seems safe, or at least safer, merely to observe that the poem shows a dissociation in Frost's mind between nature and man, and that it declines to choose one over the other.

But we have already seen that for Frost nature is fraught with the despair of a cyclic pattern of rise and fall, while at the same time the naturalist's view of life leads only rarely to wisdom, more often to a confused dereliction which spurs him to turn to intuition, humanistic aspirations. The poem assuredly records this turning from nature ("If tired of trees I seek again mankind"), but it also records a dissatisfaction with man. In "Ghost House" from the same first volume, Frost speaks of the dead as "tireless folk, but slow and sad."

> And yet, in view of how many things,
> As sweet companions as might be had.

Although "how many things" is left vague, it drifts across the consciousness as an indictment of mankind, and we ask why.

The answer is not far to seek, for the poems which derogate mankind are well known. They have a common yet misleading denominator. Two examples should suffice. In "The Flood," with an uncharacteristic cold irony Frost observes that "blood will out." The "power of blood itself releases blood." So that in war "it is once more the tidal wave / That when it has swept by leaves summits stained." Few would quarrel with the indictment. But Frost goes further. In "The Bear" he contrasts the free bear (of nature) with the caged bear, which is likened to man who

> ... sits back on his fundamental butt
> With lifted snout and eyes (if any) shut ...
> And back and forth he sways from cheek to cheek,
> At one extreme agreeing with one Greek,
> At the other agreeing with another Greek
> Which may be thought, but only so to speak.
> A baggy figure, equally pathetic
> When sedentary and when peripatetic.

Obviously enough, Frost in both poems objects to a fatal limitation in man. This limitation is the common denominator; however the limitations in the separate poems are not identical. In "The Flood" Frost deplores the excess, the violent power of man's passions which break forth to control him whether or not his reason is willing. In "The Bear," he sees reason itself as a cage, Platonic or Aristotelian, and wanting the grandeur and freedom, the instinct and passion of the uncaged bear. If one knew only these two poems he would reckon Frost a pessimist as well as so contradictory a thinker as to be irresponsible. But these are extreme poems and to a degree at least their seeming contradictions are forged together in Frost's mind. Like all extreme statements they both mislead and educate. They educate well only if they urge us to immerse ourselves in Frost's concept of the relationship of man in general to nature in general. They ask us to seek the essence of the limitations imposed by reason and by passion.

II

Though a naturalist-observer, Frost is no primitivist in the sense of admiring our dim, feral origins. He is a far more sophisticated, a far less innocent American than Melville's Captain Delano who exclaims, "There's naked nature, now; pure tenderness and love." The very orderliness of the habits of ants seems sardonically "departmental" to him—their instinct for order is akin to man's passion for impersonal organization. Animal instinct is, indeed, no constant source of awe or wonder. It is the cage of nature and fallible. Noting that the white-tailed hornet mistakes nail head and huckleberry for flies, Frost asks:

> Won't this whole instinct matter bear revision?
> Won't almost any theory bear revision?
> To err is human, not to, animal.
> Or so we pay the compliment to instinct,
> Only too liberal of our compliment
> That really takes away instead of gives.
> Our worship, humor, conscientiousness
> Went long since to the dogs under the table.
> And served us right for having instituted
> Downward comparisons. As long on earth
> As our comparisons were stoutly upward
> With gods and angels, we were men at least,
> But little lower than the gods and angels.
> But once comparisons were yielded downward,
> Once we began to see our images
> Reflected in the mud and even dust,
> 'Twas disillusion upon disillusion.
> We were lost piecemeal to the animals,
> Like people thrown out to delay the wolves.
> Nothing but fallibility was left us,
> And this day's work made even that seem doubtful.

I do not suppose that the passage needs elucidation, but we may pause to record that Frost is departing here in two ways from the general tenor of naturalistic literature since, say, 1850. The realist writer has admired instinct because it was real; the naturalist because it was natural; and the romantic because it could, like anything else, be considered shocking or thrilling; or, as in the case of Mark Twain, writers could turn to instinct as a way of avoiding the ambiguous pitfalls of the old mad dance of good and evil. Even so confirmed a humanist as E. M. Forster nods upon occasion in the direction of instinct. But Frost's observations tell him that instinctive behavior can be mean or faulty. Or, perhaps, it is reason that tells him instinct is inadequate. And perhaps it is reason also that tells him reason is inadequate. At this impasse can we only playfully withdraw, as Frost does in "To a Thinker" (who moves from one extreme position to another, from force to matter, from form to content), by saying, "But trust my instinct—I'm a bard"?

The trouble with reason, as one sees in "The Bear," is that it runs to "metaphysical extremes," which are limitations far short of wisdom and which furthermore lead to a stasis and abstraction which to Frost seem meaningless. However, when reason is pushed against nature, or (to bring the terms into line) when man's spirit is pushed against nature, the stasis and the abstract may be avoided, the world becomes neither the cage of passions and instinct nor the cage of the limited intellect. From the friction between the two, instinct and reason, comes movement, and *movement*, of course, is the freedom of the uncaged bear—only greater, for the bear is only beautiful to man the observer; he is not beautiful—at least not in the same poignant way—to the instinctual bear.

In Frost's view, the human spirit must continuously enlarge itself and contend with nature. There must be always a contest, else there is only a continuous prison whether it be the prison of nature or that of intellect. Never ripeness, but motion is all. Such a view leads him to a point where he can both deplore human action and at the same time admire it. In "A Roadside Stand" he can grieve that the country poor build an absurd roadside kiosk to plead:

> ... for some city money to feel in hand
> To try if it will not make our being expand,

And give us the life of the moving pictures' promise
That the party in power is said to be keeping from us.

Yes, they are pathetic clowns. He adds:

Sometimes I feel myself I can hardly bear
The thought of so much childish longing in vain,
The sadness that lurks near the open window there,
That waits all day in almost open prayer
For the squeal of brakes, the sound of a stopping car,
Of all the thousand selfish cars that pass,
Just one to inquire what a farmer's prices are.

But his final comment is:

I can't help owning the great relief it would be
To put these people at one stroke out of their pain.
And then next day as I come back into the sane,
I wonder how I should like you to come to me
And offer to put me gently out of my pain.

What subtle emanations rise from these laconic phrases! To put
a poet out of his pain! If these people are foolish, still they are
making a brave gesture. They may be wrong in their goal and
even in their direction, but they are right to be trying. The fact
of the matter is that Frost must, of course, admire the effort to
endure and to change, to love these things for their own sake,
as dangerous as it is to love anything for its own sake, "for what
they are." The effort is more important than success or failure.
In the poem "On a Tree Fallen Across the Road," he says the
tempest "Knows obstruction is in vain."

We will not be put off the final goal
We have it hidden in us to attain. . . .

A splendid piece of spunk—except that Frost derisively adds to
his title in parentheses: "TO HEAR US TALK." Does he
really believe, one asks, in his pep talks? The peach tree planted

in the north country may die, and "if it is destined never again to grow, / It can blame this limitless trait in the hearts of men" ("There Are Roughly Zones"). And yet in the inexorable interplay of human spirit and nature, the contest liberates even though neither side may claim a clear victory. Perhaps a clear victory would be death. In the struggle the mind is kept both free and specific, and this for Frost is victory enough. "Sand Dunes," he tells us,

> . . . are the sea made land
> To come at the fisher town,
> And bury in solid sand
> The men she could not drown.
>
> She may know cove and cape,
> But she does not know mankind
> If by any change of shape,
> She hopes to cut off mind.
>
> Men left her a ship to sink:
> They can leave her a hut as well;
> And be but more free to think
> For the one more cast-off shell.

Like other of his better poems "Sand Dunes" attains a final statement, rising from inferior poems which seem to have the purpose of grinding and polishing a concept with diatribe and humor until the truer statement is released, gleaming, from the abrasives.

III

In Robert Frost's poetry the concern with man and nature is an extension of the concern with self and nature. How may the self persist in the struggle with "the whole goddam machinery"? How may the self eschew the emptiness of abstraction, the smother of passions? Frost has had something to say about the problem for poets in his introduction to the *Collected Poems* (1949): "Our problem then is, as modern abstractionists, to have the wildness pure; to be wild with nothing to be wild about. We bring up as aberrationists, giving way to undirected associates and kicking ourselves from one chance suggestion to another in all directions as of a hot afternoon in the life of a grasshopper. Theme alone can steady us down. Just as the first mystery was how a poem could have a tune in such a straightness as meter, so the second mystery is how a poem can have wildness and at the same time a subject that shall be fulfilled." The statement is relevant, but it is confined by its primary concern with poetry. We may rest part of our weight on it, but part must rest on the more general drift of the poems. And here, in the abrasive play among the poems, there emerges, at least as a personal solution, a rather whimsical figure, the "literate farmer." (I take the term from the poem "The Literate Farmer and the Planet Venus.") This figure reveals himself at times as the clown, at times as the grotesque sage ("the tramp astrologer"), but eventually we see him as the fallible yet fulfilled man in "West Running Brook." His essential quality is that of a kinetic mind always in motion: the humorist yielding to fantasist in turn yielding to thinker. He is always in part the bright schoolboy—some patient soul ought to count Frost's references to schoolboys, college boys—the mercurial tease, the enquirer. The most notable facet of the personality, however, is the erudition, all the outdoor table talk, which seems at first glance at odds with probability. We do not associate brilliant, fantastic conversation with American farmers. And I am aware that one important critic (Yvor Winters in "The Poet as Spiritual Drifter") has questioned whether the words of the young husband in "West Running Brook" are appropriate to the character, and whether the situation is at all believable.

The question is appropriate, nor does it seem answered by the observation that the character of the literate farmer is as real as Frost's own character. However, when the literate farmer sends out his thought like a sonic signal and awaits the echo, he waits for the abstract to touch the enduring surface of nature—and to return; to return transformed. And this transformation buys a lyric intensity which perhaps diminishes the claims of realism or appropriateness. But the literate farmer has a stronger claim for acceptability. There is, after all, a tradition of the thoughtful country man in New England. Few who have lived in a New England town are unaware of examples today of the tradition. And there is the overpowering—because innocent—example of Thoreau. And Thoreau himself mentions others in an offhand manner: ". . . On a Sunday afternoon, if I had chanced to be at home, I heard the crunching of the snow made by the step of a long-headed farmer, who from far through the woods sought my house to have a social 'crack'; one of the few of his vocation who are 'men on their farms'; who donned a frock instead of a professor's gown, and is as ready to extract the moral out of church or state as to haul a load of manure from his barnyard."

The phrase itself, "literate farmer," suggests two aspects evident in the components—mind and labor. These aspects permeate Frost's whole outlook and rest upon the primary foundations of nature and intuition. We may well ask, however, having adduced a character who embodies the diversity of Frost himself, what relation this character has to the rest of humankind. After all, Frost is a poet not because he is affected by nature or because he has lived on a farm, but because he speaks to men about men.

IV

Limited by certain aristocratic humors, but vantaged by tolerance, the literate farmer seeks through body and mind, through labor and contemplation to reach his fellow man while preserving at the same time his independence. The effort requires some jockeying back and forth. His intention would seem to be that of grinding together the extremes of self and society until these extremes crumble. He desires a compromise and supposes that in a commonsense view such a compromise is most apt to flourish. Perhaps no philosophic success greets the desire, but poetic successes mark the effort.

As a naturalist Frost accepts the world's evidence for as long as he can. As a naturalist he champions motion and practicality for as long as it will satisfy. The literate farmer finds a pure, but, as we shall see, a too narrow joy in the natural movement and practicality of labor.

The early poem "Mowing" is noteworthy. Frost asks what the scythe whispers, and the only answer, though for a moment one anticipates mere fantasy, remains stern, even cold: "Anything more than the truth would have seemed too weak." And indeed "The fact is the sweetest dream that labor knows." Very well, then, *fact*, but one is instantly aware that this is fact for its own sake. It is a fact well on the way to becoming a generalization; it is motion becoming abstraction. Nevertheless, the poem does show that for Frost work is a form of beauty, a beauty transfigured by a passion both absurd and profound. For example, can we say whether it is a practical interest in crops or an aesthetic rapture which kindles that little masterpiece "Putting in the Seed"?

> How Love burns through the Putting in the Seed
> On through the watching for that early birth
> When, just as the soil tarnishes with weed,
> The sturdy seedling with arched body comes
> Shouldering its way and shedding the earth crumbs.

The world's poetry contains few lines more "accurate" than these, yet they are not by any means Frost's best. Not that they are too simple (the sensuousness is awesomely complex) but that they are too simply based. Frost yields to the short view, to the partial truth. The result is quite beautiful, but because it ignores the greater strain, the grander honesty of his quarrel with nature, one does not have the impression so much of human engagement as of animal surrender. At the least, however, we obtain a clear picture of the extreme, if not the complete position which equates work and beauty—fact and sweetest truth.

This same extreme view, which elsewhere creates a Yahoo among poets (as in "At Woodward's Gardens") creates also Frost's fascination with tools, all those axes, scythes, grindstones, buzz saws. The fascination is sometimes happy, sometimes lugubrious; something of both—and something else besides—appear in "The Ax-Helve." The literate farmer is interrupted in his wood cutting by Baptiste, who deplores the machine-made ax-helve and offers to supply a good one. Part of the poem reads like a government pamphlet on ax-helves. But at the end we find that the helve, the *fact*, is a basis for understanding between the French Canadian and the farmer. One qualification emerges in the last lines:

> But now he brushed the shavings from his knee
> And stood the ax there on its horse's hoof,
> Erect, but not without its waves, as when
> The snake stood up for evil in the Garden,—
> Top-heavy with a heaviness his short,
> Thick hand made light of, steel-blue chin drawn down
> And in a little—a French touch in that.
> Baptiste drew back and squinted at it, pleased;
> 'See how she's cock her head!'

One does not take the allusion to the snake seriously. The poem is nowhere quite serious. I do, however, find that the allusion affects the ultimate tone, that it casts an amused doubt on the ax-helve as a true basis for understanding. Then, looking back over the poem one may find that the doubt is implied in another way:

> Do you know, what we talked about was knowledge?
> Baptiste on his defense about the children
> He kept from school, or did his best to keep—

Whatever school and children and our doubts
Of laid-on education had to do
With the curves of his ax-helves and his having
Used these unscrupulously to bring me
To see for once the inside of his house.
Was I desired in friendship, partly as someone
To leave it to, whether the right to hold
Such doubts of education should depend
Upon the education of those who held them?

One can scarcely say that Frost is judging Baptiste's views, but one can say that whereas the two can meet over the beauty of hickory grain and the proper use of that wood, uncertainty arises over their ability to understand each other when the concern is less tangible. The limited man and the literate farmer understand each other perfectly when the subject is as limited as craftsmanship. But it is not enough.

The matter comes to a head in the anthology piece "Two Tramps in Mud Time." The poem is curiously organized; one might almost say that it is badly organized. Almost half the poem would seem to be mere season and scene, relevant only if the reader is lenient. Nevertheless, within the whole body of Frost's poetry, "Two Tramps in Mud Time" seems an inevitability. It had to be written somewhere along the line. It begins where much of Frost's poetry begins, with an observation of the transient aspect of nature. Everything shimmers on the knife edge of a perishing moment. This is that condition of mutability which can lead Frost to an elegiac expression of the tears of things or to an amazed comprehension of the great joy of things caught, however briefly, on a pinpoint of time. Mutability is that aspect of nature which Frost sees most validly and which, therefore, most readily releases his vision. Mutability, therefore, most properly permeates the most metaphysical of Frost's perceptions of beauty. Yet not every note struck can aspire *ad astra*. On a very human plane, physical labor is, as I have been at pains to point out, associated in

Frost's mind with beauty. "Two Tramps in Mud Time" brings both the theme of mutability and the theme of the beauty of labor together, so that this is "the time when most I loved my task," when the season is plangent with the uncertainty of everything. And the task has a rough feel, a brute release. The "two hulking tramps," more limited than Baptiste,

> judged me by their appropriate tool.
> Except as a fellow handled an ax,
> They had no way of knowing a fool.

Frost agrees that "theirs was the better right." They need work; he merely "loves" the work. Yet he goes on to claim didactically for himself a "higher" if not "better" right.

> My object in living is to unite
> My avocation and my vocation
> As my two eyes make one in sight,
> Only where love and need are one,
> And the work is play for mortal stakes,
> Is the deed ever really done
> For Heaven and the future's sakes.

Although the poem is so explicit that there is hardly any question of meaning, one is drawn to compare the position with that in "Mowing" and "The Tuft of Flowers." What in "Two Tramps in Mud Time" has happened to the fact, the sweetest truth? And are men working together really? The fact has become theory, it has started up the ladder pointed toward heaven, and it is clear that the two tramps are not inclined to follow. They are working toward a different, a limited goal. The happy notion of men working together whether they will or not, the happy notion in "The Tuft of Flowers" will not hold up, then, always for Frost. It is true only so long as the objective is superficial and momentary. Or, more importantly, it is true that men work together only if the objective is not practical; if it is a flower to be spared, yes; if a belly is to be fed

—perhaps no. These poems gather together because they are concerned with trying to find a mode of understanding between people. The fact-work-beauty association is a step, not a false one, but not a final one.

Reconsider the poems "After Apple-Picking" and "The Wood-Pile." In the first of these, Frost is tired of the harvest he desired. The practical harvest has the effect of numbing him, so that he begins to drift into a dream state which is the antithesis of the practical. In "The Wood-Pile" he contrasts the human, practical purpose of a woodpile with the obscure purpose of "the slow, smokeless burning of decay." In both, fact and practicality are diminished virtues. And if these foundations crumble, is it very surprising to find him probing from a different direction altogether? Sometimes, indeed, he considers the lilies of the field.

V

Although Frost tends to value work for its own sake, or for an aesthetic sake, his obverse tendency to value impracticality or uselessness seems an embarrassment. It is a bit awkward, seeming to suggest an abandonment of his hope to meet and understand others through work, through the wordlessness of the physical world. But let us see.

At the simplest level a comparison of "The Tuft of Flowers" and "Rose Pogonias" is instructive. In the former, the flowers have been spared by another worker. "In Rose Pogonias" there is the prayer

> That none should mow the grass there
> While so confused with flowers.

To be sure, "Rose Pogonias" is not a weighty poem. It depends very largely on a charming but small conceit—these little orchid flowers appear to grow on spears of grass. And it arrives at its delicate destination by asking that the gentle and useless beauty be spared by the practical mowers. A similar mood imbues "Unharvested":

> May something go always unharvested!
> May much stay out of our stated plan,
> Apples or something forgotten and left,
> So smelling their sweetness would be no theft.

Or, "A Young Birch," loved for its beauty alone, so that

> The most efficient help you ever hired
> Would know that it was there to be admired,
> And zeal would not be thanked that cut it down
> When you were reading books or out of town.
> It was a thing of beauty and was sent
> To live its life out as an ornament.

The theme of the sacredness of useless beauty in these modest poems becomes a tour de force in "New Hampshire," amused and amusing but hardly golden. Neither modest nor tour de force is the neglected and very superior poem "An Encounter." The poem works several of Frost's cherished motives into the fabric; these seem perhaps less integral to the poem than significant of the depth of association, the fullness of experience that the poem imparts. It opens by playing the theme of mutability: the day is a "weather breeder." The poet is once again withdrawn into the woods and confronted by the frequent accompaniment of such withdrawal:

> Choked with oil of cedar
> And scurf of plants, and weary and over-heated,
> And sorry I ever left the road I knew

Then the ambiguous and half-hearted impulse toward heaven appears:

> I paused and rested on a sort of hook
> That had me by the coat as good as seated,

> And since there was no other way to look,
> Looked up toward heaven . . .

This time, however, not a birch tree nor a ladder. He is resting against a telephone pole.

> 'You here?' I said. 'Where aren't you nowadays?
> And tell me what's the news you carry—if you know?
> And tell me where you're off for—Montreal?

Then in answer to an implied question from the pole:

> Me? I'm not off for anywhere at all.
> Sometimes I wander out of beaten ways
> Half looking for the orchid Calypso.

If one looks beneath the surface of the poem here is what he finds. The literate farmer has withdrawn from engagement in the world (compare "A Drumlin Woodchuck"); he has ceased to try to communicate with man either with words or through ax-helves or cutter bars. Yet what he discovers in the wilderness is the communication par excellence of the telephone. And he is made aware of the practical, the ruthlessly utilitarian motivation of the circumambient civilization. It is going somewhere. It thinks it has something to say. Yet he stands ironically still, insisting on his right to be going nowhere in particular, and to have no purpose beyond "half looking for the orchid Calypso." And when one realizes that this orchid has been virtually extinct in New England for many years, he realizes to what degree Frost is championing the virtue of uselessness.

Clearly, one has to acknowledge a gap between Frost's love of fact, work, and use and his love of aimless inutility. These contradictory urgencies ironically derive from the same center, from a desire to stand with and to understand others. Through dynamic movement he seeks to enter and belong to the world; through withdrawal he seeks to nourish and assert the self. He must have both and perhaps earns them by sweating so fastidiously.

SIX

Thanks to the Human Heart

I suppose that one ought to consider the poem "Mending Wall" as the most important of Frost's utterances on the score of the relationship between men, communication. Certainly the temptation is great. Granted, important ingredients abide in the poem, and it is well known and popular. But "Mending Wall" is, despite its undeniable immediacy and charm, rather distracted. The tone slants toward an inappropriate shrillness with the early references to hunters who "have left not one stone on a stone, / But they would have the rabbit out of hiding, / To please the yelping dogs." The poem never quite recovers from this false step. The images are at best only workaday ("The boulders ... are loaves and some so nearly balls"). Finally there is so much one-sided humor, one part malicious and two parts vapid, that as I read the poem I have the picture of the narrator chortling to himself somewhat crazily as he fondles the stones. Frost's humor is only really effective when by being largely self-satire it escapes the danger of seeming self-righteous. At any rate, to read "Mending Wall" as a plea for breaking down traditional barriers, for breaking down the past conventions takes us to a position which nothing else in Frost's poetry supports. Nor does "Mending Wall" successfully support such a position, for the poet-narrator himself cooperates with the wall-builder, replacing the stones in the spring even as he protests in spirit.

Ultimately, Frost prefers to let the way of man's relation to man fall to chance—or to a faith in some kind of spontaneous understanding. The contemplative lyrics, however, do not give a complete picture, for they primarily reveal a personal experience, an environment of yield and reluctance wherein Frost is agonist. The contemplative lyrics differ somewhat from those directly given to narrative or dramatic aims. To be sure, most of Frost's poems are dramatically *arranged*—they have a plot, supported by a linguistic intrigue, accident, change, and realization; but I have in mind poems dealing with characters more nearly separate from Frost himself. These must be added to the lyrics in judging his view of man's relationship to man.

When I separate the narrative poems from the lyrics I do not deny that his idiom and outlook are omnipresent. The experience in the narratives, however, is usually *extra*-Frost. The experience does not crystallize from the laws of Frost's being. "The Death of the Hired Man," "The Generations of Men," "The Housekeeper," "The Fear," "The Self-Seeker," to name only a few, presumably do not reflect anything which ever happened to Frost directly. They have been heard from others, perhaps; or, somewhat less likely, they have been observed. Whatever the fact, these stories require that Frost supply motivations and articulation appropriate to viewpoints other than his own. For Frost, who, with the sure ear of a master, can establish absolutely his own smile-struck grief in a phrase, a word, this requirement seems to be a very great task. Certainly, the moment he permits himself to enter the poem as "I," the important spectator and immediate narrator, no other character has much of a chance, and even though the poem offers a story, it does not then tell a story—it becomes, as in "The Star-Splitter," amused gossip or, as in "The Black Cottage," narrative enclosure for a monologue. Herein is no disadvantage put upon these poems. They realize themselves in other than narrative ways. But it does suggest that Frost is not innately a storyteller. (Neither was Mark Twain and for a similar reason.) When I read, as I have recently, that Frost is to be compared with Chaucer, I am aghast. No one was ever more interested in a story for the story's sake than Chaucer; no one less interested in the story for the story's sake than Frost. Yet he has written narrative poems, and while I cannot wholeheartedly admire them as examples of narrative art I can admire many of them on other grounds. They hurt me with their kindness or their cruelty and most of them reveal an idiosyncrasy at once notable and instructive. As typical of the best "The Death of the Hired Man" may serve as example.

No argument need rise about the poem's emotional properties. The portrait does touch the heart. Silas' stubborn human worth survives his worthlessness. His loyalty to his one competence—building a load of hay—triumphs over his fickleness. And all this made sharp by terms suited to the environment. Touching enough and sharp enough, indeed, to make it seem treachery to ask for more than is given. Yet to probe the outlines is not treachery. And if one does probe he will find that the whole management of characters is a little like a game of skittles; that is, the characters are propelled into an environment where after the initial momentum they simply move according to natural law. They are "accomplished" characters apparently, incapable of change. Mary pleads with Warren to be as "kind" as she is. Warren, in asking Mary to be less tender-hearted, is asking her to be like himself. Silas, one gathers, has always been as he is. Even in the reminiscence of his argument with a "college boy" we find unyielding attitudes; neither will change. At the end, the only alteration is the purely physical one of death. Now, inasmuch as all these characters do not change, do not yield, they are, or seem to be, incapable of learning. In all truth "The Death of the Hired Man" is almost meaningless for the reader since it is meaningless for the characters.

The same conflict of obdurate selves characterizes "The Code," where we seem to be proffered a kind of theme:

> The hand that knows his business won't be told
> To do work better or faster . . .

The dramatization of this theme takes the form of a hired man's reminiscence of being irritated by his employer's eagerness for work, especially

If by so doing he could get more work
Out of his hired help.

Hence when

 ...the old fool seizes his fork in both hands,
And looking up bewhiskered out of the pit,
Shouts like an army captain, "Let her come!"
Thinks I, D'ye mean it? "What was that you said?"
I asked out loud, so's there'd be no mistake,
"Did you say, Let her come?" "Yes, let her come."
He said it over, but he said it softer.
Never you say a thing like that to a man,
Not if he values what he is. God, I'd as soon
Murdered him as left out his middle name.
I'd built the load and knew right where to find it.
Two or three forkfuls I picked lightly round for
Like meditating, and then I just dug in
And dumped the rackful on him in ten lots.
I looked over the side once in the dust
And caught sight of him treading-water-like,
Keeping his head above. "Damn ye," I says,
"That gets ye!" He squeaked like a squeezed rat.
That was the last I saw or heard of him.

The man is not, however, smothered to death, and the poem
finishes:

'Weren't you relieved to find he wasn't dead?'

'No! and yet I don't know—it's hard to say.
I went about to kill him fair enough.'

'You took an awkward way. Did he discharge you?'

'Discharge me? No! He knew I did just right.'

[79   ]

To be sure, one finds an ironical insight in the poem; still every character ends pretty much as he began. The feeling of sameness holds less true for "The Fear," which ebbs and flows with psychological interest, but it holds generally true of the narratives which turn on an overt conflict of view or bias.

The result of the immutability of character is that we have character sketches, people finished before they are begun, a geometric configuration of characters rather than dynamic development. Possibly for this very reason, Frost's "The Witch of Coös," which conforms with exquisite docility to a tradition of supernatural tales, may seem more real, more refractive than "The Death of the Hired Man." Because he seems naturally to conceive of character as perfected—that is, unchangeable—Frost tends in his narratives to present a waxworks allegory. There they are: jelled, posed, frozen. This static view of character lies beneath Frost's tendency to reject tragic demonstration and resolution. And more than that, the rejection of tragedy (or the inability to apprehend it) makes his two closet dramas "A Masque of Reason" (1945) and "A Masque of Mercy" (1947), rather anomalous if not self-defeating.

"A Masque of Reason" develops as a commentary on that terrifying drama, the Book of Job, which for all its happy ending remains the most tragic of dramas for the reason that the happy ending is itself an illumination of the impotence of man to manage his own destiny or even to comprehend the forces which manage it for him. Satan, the adversary of man, who here in blinding moments seems less an adversary than does God, is in the Book of Job not at all God's adversary but his helper. Despite the odds the Biblical Job strains for comprehension, he argues with God and changes during the course of the drama from a righteous, wealthy man to a subliminal essence of righteousness for its own obscure sake. But the cost is only short of too much; altogether too much for the ordinary mortal. When Frost reshapes the story he has God revisit Job in a quasi-modern world. God, whom Job's wife says she would recognize anywhere "by Blake's picture," tells Job:

> My thanks are to you for releasing me
> From moral bondage to the human race.
> The only free will there at first was man's,
> Who could do good or evil as he chose.
> I had no choice but I must follow him
> With forfeits and rewards he understood—
> Unless I liked to suffer loss of worship.
> I had to prosper good and punish evil.
> You changed all that. You set me free to reign.
> You are the Emancipator of your God,
> And as such I promote you to a saint.

It is all very well for Frost in other poems to tease his reader or to tease his characters, but Frost's God ought to be greater than Frost. He ought not to tease, ought not to lose His divinity. And Job's reply:

> You hear him, Thyatira: we're a saint.
> Salvation in our case is retroactive.
> We're saved, we're saved, whatever else it means.

This reply, surely, must be described not as humor but as kidding, and it gives us a Job not merely wanting in dignity but wanting, in any high sense, humanity as well. For now it becomes all a practical joke. Is it Job or Petroleum Nasby who speaks?

> You perhaps will tell us
> If that is all there is to be of heaven,
> Escape from so great pains of life on earth
> It gives a sense of let-up calculated
> To last a fellow to Eternity.

On such notes, which are not grace notes, all the haunting enormity of the trial of Job mutates into the cheap fooling around of *The Green Pastures.* (Have a five cent seegah, Lord.) I confess as a matter of fairness that I am irrationally prejudiced against the modern tendency to debase myth and religion by sieving it through anthropology and mystagogy and spreading it thin upon a modern setting: Cocteau, Gide. But I prefer this perversion to Frost's conversion of high seriousness to serious comedy.

I cannot but feel much the same way about Frost's modernist commentary on the Jonah story, "A Masque of Mercy." Too much of the same debunking tone prevails, although justice compels the observation that it obtains interest and worth from counterpoising New Testament mercy and Old Testament vengefulness. To a degree, perhaps, "A Masque of Mercy" attempts to set straight the impossible irresolution of the Job story: "Nothing can make injustice just but mercy." Yet in this very counterpoising Frost again denies the fury of life and the tragic muse. In fact the denial becomes almost too literal and certainly too literary:

> Jonah: What's all this talk of slaying down in cellars—
> So sinister? You spoke to someone down there.
>
> Keeper: My friends and stokers, Jeffers and O'Neill.
> They fail me. Now I'm teasing you again.
> There's no one down there getting tortured save
> A penitent perhaps self-thrown on Mercy.

Somewhere I have read that the masques are examples of "Yankee humor" and that they may offend the "orthodox." They may be examples of Yankee humor (though I know of no other similar examples), but the phrase, if it describes, hardly excuses. I cannot speak for the orthodox, but I should think most sensitive readers might be distressed for an entirely simple reason: Frost's masques are meaningless without reference to the Biblical originals, and once these originals are brought to mind, the discrepancy between the earnest and the flip is painful; the difference between the cosmic drama and Yankee humor is unnerving. If one is going to re-do the great myths he had better do so in a spirit of equivalent seriousness, as did Milton or Shelley. If he cannot do this, then let him invent new stories, else he commits sacrilege—not against a religion—but, in asking us to substitute the trivial for the great, the genial for the true—a sacrilege against the spirit of mankind.

We have come to that which underlies the only important shortcoming of Frost's poetry. Too often he supposes that to save himself from appearing a fool he must prove himself a wise man. Too often he pursues no lover's quarrel with the world but only a casual flirtation with the reader. Too often he ignores the serious implications of his own poems. They move toward a devastating synergy only to be stopped short, deformed in a joke or deformed in one of Frost's infuriatingly skillful asides or brilliant understatements. Skillful or brilliant, such poems stop short of victory. One would not be so unkind as to press this if he felt that Frost were incapable of finishing the race; if he really felt that Frost always has to stop just before breasting the tape in order to turn and wave at the grandstand. But on the basis of a handful of great poems—the anger rises because there might have been more—one knows that the limitation sometimes at least is willfully, almost coldly imposed. Why?

I cannot answer my question, but I can complicate it. In 1917 Frost printed a short play, *A Way Out*, which was given an amateur performance at the Academy of Music of Northampton, Massachusetts, in 1919. *A Way Out* is a very strange play. The idiom throughout is the idiom of all of Frost's colloquial poetry. The attitudes—these, too, are Frost's—are attitudes which one only suspects or sees so fleetingly in the poems that it seems almost prudent to ignore them.

The play runs this way: Old Asa Gorrill (who is certainly no kind of gorilla) since the death of his brother has lived alone in his farmhouse. At the time the play opens, Asa receives a stranger who quickly lets it be known that he is a murderer and a fugitive from a pursuing posse. The murderer is imperiously virile and wickedly aware of life. He may seem finally a more admirable character than Asa. His contemptuous comment makes justice: "I've heard of you and your brother keeping old maid's hall over here in this neck of the woods, patching each other's trousers and doing up each other's back hair." And Asa, as he discovers that he harbors a criminal, is both frightened and morbidly fascinated. The stranger plans, it would seem, to hide in Asa's house, passing himself off as Asa should anyone come by. He dons some of Asa's clothing and then forces Asa into holding hands with him and whirling as in a child's game until they shall grow dizzy and fall. "And then when we're down," he says, "I want you should wait till you can see straight before you speak and try to tell which is which and which is t'other." But, of course, after they fall moaning to the floor, each accuses the other of being Cain. Though the play suggests that the murderer then strikes Asa and drags him from the room, returning in time to pass himself off to the arriving posse as Asa Gorrill, one still feels that perhaps Asa himself has instead suddenly thought of himself as a murderer and hence become one. The play, then, by traversing the thin line between good and evil and by forcing the reader to believe that not only are these extremes barely separate in an abstract sense, but that they are furthermore at home within one person, leads us to the margin of moral terror, to that moment of mocking knowledge when we see suddenly the meekest and most ordinary face as only a glaze upon murder. I gather that some such experience comes, albeit rarely, to very sensitive people and that it comes as a horrifying discovery, an inverted vision illuminating not the unity of all things with God but the desolate separation of all things in evil. To Hawthorne the vision came as regularly as the tides. It moves Young Goodman Brown and Mr. Dimmesdale and even Major Molineux's kinsman, Robin, to demonic hysteria, spiritual inebriation, where they laugh with fiends. The laughter is without rationality, without humor.

It is strange that Frost should have censored this insight in himself. Not only has he seemed to discourage discussion of the play, but he has never permitted himself to return to the vision. Yet he must have experienced such an intuition or it would never at any time have occurred to him to write about it. It is not synthetic, this vision. Yet he has blocked the nerve. As I confessed I can only enrich the question, but if I do not know why he chose deliberately to bar himself from the expression of a profound insight, still I am aware that something lies beneath all this. To have once had such a vision is to have it forever. There is no ridding oneself of it except by ridding oneself of memory or by changing one's whole life. If Frost has not given full voice to his awareness of the jest and riddle, he has nevertheless not lost the awareness. He has covered it. It emerges from time to time to bring a sudden richness and altogether surprising manner to his poetry. On the one hand one might wish for more of it, yet to be just he must on the other hand admit that Frost has avoided stridency and pretentiousness better than any other important poet of the twentieth century and that perhaps he has been able to for the reason that he has carefully guarded his most dangerous mood. For where the vision does arise it is transmuted; fair metal, no dross, no tell-tale matrix. It arises without commitment to optimism or pessimism, without commitment to fad or slogan, almost without commitment to attitude or belief, yet committed finally to what I would call a purified seriousness.

The fullest expression of the vision comes rarely, but there are rumors here and there. A few examples: In one of his strangest and least believable poems, "Into My Own," Frost laments that "those dark trees" are "the merest mask of gloom," instead of stretching "away unto the edge of doom." He continues:

> I should not be withheld but that some day
> Into their vastness I should steal away,
> Fearless of ever finding open land,
> Or highway where the slow wheel pours the sand.

I do not see why I should e'er turn back
Or those should not set forth upon my track
To overtake me, who should miss me here
And long to know if still I held them dear.

They would not find me changed from him they knew—
Only more sure of all I thought was true.

The thing that is troubling about the poem is that it begins
by emphasizing through rhyme and dramatic placement the
notion of "doom," but progresses instead only to his characteristic retreat from the beaten path into the pathless wilderness.
Yet the coloration of the "doom" persists through the terminal
couplet to link, however weakly, the discovery of self with
something fateful, something even eschatological.

Again, the sonnet "Design," which asks us to observe a white
spider holding its prey, a white moth on a white flower, the
heal-all.

A snow-drop spider, a flower like a froth,
And dead wings carried like a paper kite.

And then:

What had that flower to do with being white,
The wayside blue and innocent heal-all?
What brought the kindred spider to that height,
Then steered the white moth thither in the night?
What but design of darkness to appall?
If design govern in a thing so small.

The poem is a footnote to Melville's Maldive shark; the
strangeness of the charming blue flower's albino form becomes
in its chill abnormality a kill-all. But the last line, "If design
govern in a thing so small," simultaneously confirms and
tries to change the effect of the metaphysical fear. To change
the terror by suggesting that the universe perhaps does not
sanction such a cruel and cannibal intersection, that it is ac-

cident rather than intent; to confirm the terror, however, by the implication that there may be no design for anything whether great or small, nothing but an ash-white plain without love or faith or hope, where ignorant appetites cross by chance.

There is a common pattern in the two poems "Into My Own" and "Design," a pattern even more patently revealed in one of Frost's most brilliant poems, "Provide, Provide." Swinging gracefully and sturdily through its triplet rhymes, the poem tells of "the beauty Abishag," once "The picture pride of Hollywood" who has fallen "from great and good" to become a "withered hag," a scrub woman. The poem offers double advice:

> Die early and avoid the fate
> Or if predestined to die late,
> Make up your mind to die in state.
>
> . . . .
>
> No memory of having starred
> Atones for later disregard,
> Or keeps the end from being hard.
>
> Better to go down dignified
> With boughten friendship at your side
> Than none at all. Provide, provide!

The genesis of the poem is the memory of a college (Frost attended Dartmouth and Harvard) where the dormitory charwomen were so poorly paid that the undergraduates conducted a strike in their behalf. The actuality, through the addition of Abishag who has risen high and fallen low, is transformed into a little spoof-tragedy. The aphoristic advice is certainly ambivalent. The first injunction—to die early—is usual enough. We get it all the way down the line from the Greeks to Housman. It is a reverso way of saying that to fulfill yourself you must spring as soon as possible into the waiting arms of your tragedy. But the other injunction, to buy friendship and so forth, is the antithesis of destiny, tragedy.

Now, it must immediately be confessed that this observation violates the ground rules of Frost's poem, fails to acknowledge the grimness and the skew smile. The grimness and the smile are there and may in the final analysis make us more aware of pathetic irony than of anything else. Yet if one can abstract flat statement from the leaven of the whole, it is as I have pointed out—that here as in "Into My Own" and "Design" we receive a glimpse of final things followed by a reconsideration and finally an adoption of an anti-tragic view. In "Into My Own" one probably feels divided and dissatisfied with the retrenchment. In "Design," because the retrenchment turns suddenly, destructively upon itself, one may feel that the poem re-gathers its uncertainty to a unity. In "Provide, Provide" he may feel that the technical ardor and the cool fear finally circumscribe the poem with illumination. The latter two poems are, heaven knows, anything but failures. They are among Frost's finest. Yet they are fine because they give us a glimpse of profound honesty just before it is obscured. And in the lesser poems we do not see the rejection and denial honestly represented. We do not see the interplay of strain and trial, actuality and aspiration. There is only a mild blindness, a spongy tractability. That Frost is aware of an imposed boundary that he *chooses* rather than *prefers* (he chooses the mask of gloom, not the edge of doom) seems documented in "For Once, Then, Something."

> Others taunt me with having knelt at well-curbs
> Always wrong to the light, so never seeing
> Deeper down in the well than where the water
> Gives me back in a shining surface picture
> Me myself in the summer heaven godlike
> Looking out of a wreath of fern and cloud puffs.

But he insists that *once* he saw "Something more of the depths—and then I lost it":

One drop fell from a fern, and lo, a ripple
Shook whatever it was lay there at bottom,
Blurred it, blotted it out. What was that whiteness?
Truth? A pebble of quartz? For once, then, something.

Only once? No, that is not true. We have too many examples that strike deep, deeper indeed than this poem with its
evasive defense. In addition we have those poems which instead
of offering one way or two ways out of the blanched garden,
glance steadily and then move on to convert the experience to
what I have already referred to as a purified seriousness. I
consider it the triumph of a true Frost over a half-false Frost,
a triumph of a stern art over a half-soft rationalization. The
brilliant half-life of an unstable element yielding finally to
the lithic definition of the stable element. That it happens
rarely does not challenge the importance nor does it become
in the long run any less inevitable. Humankind can bear more
reality than Prufrock supposes, but it can seldom attain it.

I would propose two examples, finally, of a purified seriousness in Frost's poetry, "The Black Cottage" and "West Run-
ning-Brook." The former draws upon materials precious to
Frost: The cottage is deserted and also haunted by its former
life; the cottage, like the woodpile, is decaying; the woman who
had lived there had stubbornly resisted fad and change, cyni-
cism and topical absurdity:

She had some art of hearing and yet not
Hearing the latter wisdom of the world.
White was the only race she ever knew.
Black she had scarcely seen, and yellow never.
But how could they be made so very unlike
By the same hand working in the same stuff?
She had supposed the war decided that.
What are you going to do with such a person?
Strange how such innocence gets its own way.

I shouldn't be surprised if in this world
It were the force that would at last prevail.

The minister who tells her story observes that he "would
have changed the Creed a very little" in order "to please the
younger members of the church" except that it would have
too much startled her. The language of the first part of the
poem is typical of Frost's dramatic monologues—literate and
colloquial at the same time. But suddenly toward the end the
language alters and rises to a rhetoric that is openly noble, as
stirring and true as only English blank verse can be. And like all
great poetry it arises from having looked into the depths of
experience and then made up its mind. I mean seriously that
the poetry rather than the author makes up its mind and in so
doing virtuously dedicates itself to the intellectual history—
therefore the glory—of mankind:

'I'm just as glad she made me keep hands off,
For, dear me, why abandon a belief
Merely because it ceases to be true.
Cling to it long enough, and not a doubt
It will turn true again, for so it goes.
Most of the change we think we see in life
Is due to truths being in and out of favor.
As I sit here, and often times, I wish
I could be monarch of a desert land
I could devote and dedicate forever
To the truths we keep coming back and back to.
So desert it would have to be, so walled
By mountain ranges half in summer snow,
No one would covet it or think it worth
The pains of conquering to force change on.
Scattered oases where men dwelt, but mostly
Sand dunes held loosely in tamarisk
Blown over and over themselves in idleness.

Sand grains should sugar in the natal dew
The babe born to the desert, the sand storm
Retard mid-waste my cowering caravans—
There are bees in this wall.' He struck the clapboards,
Fierce heads looked out; small bodies pivoted.
We rose to go. Sunset blazed on the windows.

This poem brings us the victory over impermanency which
comes only from gazing earnestly at change. "West-Running
Brook" offers an equal triumph, and it is a riper, greater poem.
My final chapter has the aim of trying to say how great.

SEVEN

West-Running Brook

Beginning with the second mature volume *North of Boston*, a pattern of fantasy willfully counterweighed against reality emerges in Frost's poems. One reader may glide over the fantasy as charming playfulness; of course, to a degree it is. Another reader may check, finding the fantasy insincere or even silly. Whether charming or silly, the pattern leads to matters more important than the pattern itself is.

Examples are not hard to come by, but it is noteworthy that among the most evident are Frost's best-known poems: "Mending Wall," "After Apple-Picking," "The Wood-Pile," "Birches," and "West-Running Brook." In "Mending Wall" "the frozen-ground swell . . . spills the upper boulders in the sun." Or hunters leave "not one stone on a stone." Very well, these are causes. Yet behind the first of these lies a presumptive insistence: "Something there is that does not love a wall." How explain these gaps that no one sees made? How, indeed, can he explain to his neighbor the metaphysical belief which underlies the poem? The neighbor could not believe or accept the generalization. "I could say 'Elves' to him,/ But it's not elves exactly, and I'd rather/ He said it for himself." Let us examine this pattern further.

Frost gives three causes for the event: the real or natural cause (frost heave), the "metaphysical" (something) cause which Frost feels ought to enclose or include the first cause as well as the event itself, and, finally, the fantastic cause (elves) offered whimsically; whimsically, yes, but still as if it were a necessary gesture, a way of satisfying a stubborn viewpoint.

In "After Apple-Picking," the experience of harvest turns

into a lovely punishment with the synaptic echoing and re-echoing of the experience: "Magnified apples appear and disappear." And:

> My instep arch not only keeps the ache,
> I feel the ladder sway as the boughs bend.

The experience is without question psychologically true and finely detailed. And yet, it is all introduced *as if* it were the result of a fantastic cause:

> I cannot rub the strangeness from my sight
> I got from looking through a pane of glass
> I skimmed this morning from the drinking trough.

We take this as an accidental parallel to the later details, but we can hardly take it as true cause. Are we then to see it as a little joke? Any answer of this question must take into account the whole poem, which at bottom sadly wonders about what I suppose we must nowadays call the hoarding instinct. The pseudo-cause, the fantasy of the pane of ice, buffers the sad wonder, half denies the mortally ironic exhaustion. Not, however, because it is a little joke but because it asserts the particularity of a personal view.

Again in "The Wood-Pile," though the poem moves toward a serious image, the whole poem moves, quite literally, by following the flight of a small bird who "was careful

> To put a tree between us when he lighted,
> And say no word to tell me who he was
> Who was so foolish as to think what *he* thought.
> He thought that I was after him for a feather—
> The white one in his tail, like one who takes
> Everything said as personal to himself.

It is this droll creature who, by going behind the woodpile "to make his last stand," brings to the poet's eye the real poem. There is such great contrast between bird and the woodpile's

[93]

"Slow smokeless burning of decay" that it becomes difficult to say whether the direction of the poem is profoundly innocent or profoundly contrived. No matter. The bird's egocentric motivation surrenders surprisingly to the impersonal awareness of the last lines, and one assumes that the purpose of the whimsical direction is neither contrast nor parallel but rather a loosening of insight. It is as if for Frost the direct or immediate truth or cause has only ordinary consequences, and only when it is brought into a rich doubt by fantasy can the imagination leap across the chain of ordinary cause and effect to arrive at a far goal.

All of this is climactic in a more famous poem. If one were a strict formalist I suspect he would have to confess that "Birches" is neither a precise nor an economical poem. However, the theme is ably presented in the last third of the poem:

> It's when I'm weary of considerations,
> And life is too much like a pathless wood
> Where your face burns and tickles with the cobwebs
> Broken across it, and one eye is weeping
> From a twig's having lashed across it open.
> I'd like to get away from earth awhile
> And then come back to it and begin over.
> May no fate willfully misunderstand me
> And half grant what I wish and snatch me away
> Not to return. Earth's the right place for love:
> I don't know where it's likely to go better.
> I'd like to go by climbing a birch tree,
> And climb black branches up a snow-white trunk
> *Toward* heaven, till the tree could bear no more,
> But dipped its top and set me down again.
> That would be good both going and coming back.
> One could do worse than be a swinger of birches.

The theme of having divine pie and eating it too needs no particular explanation, but the proportioning of the whole poem does. Roughly two-thirds of "Birches" is given to the "true" reasons for the bent trees as against the wishful or willful reasons, that is to say, ice storms versus some solitary boy "too far from town to learn baseball,/ Whose only play was what he found himself,/ Summer or winter, and could play alone." Frost's preference goes to the nostalgic fantasy, the reason as it might humanly and beautifully exist, but "Truth" breaks in, and truth must have her due. One may well pause to ask what connection the discrepancy between reality and fantasy has to do with the conclusion. In all faith I do not think there is any but a verbal one. Furthermore, I see no very great reason for caring. I have reservations about "Birches," but the want of logical relation is not primary among them. If the poem is loosely co-ordinated it is nevertheless natural. If it denies art it does not refuse nature. But my purpose is to point out how easily the quarrel between reality and the as-if fantasy intrudes upon the poem. Why should this be? The truth is that Frost would like nature to concur with human intuition more than it is ever willing to do. Such an aspiration poses a dilemma. Frost's dilemma is that of an American transcendentalism which would if it could, find in nature (of all places!) the equivalences, indeed identities, of civilized hopes. By virtue of a soft Platonism, the dilemma did not really present itself to Emerson, but Hawthorne, who at every turn suggests that appearances are misleading, was stricken by the ambiguities. Melville worked so hard to unify the two that he all but destroyed the civilized hope. Twain tried to soothe the trouble by shifting the terms, though not the essential meaning, from "nature" to "experience." It did not work. For while Twain could feel the necessity for counterpoising experience against illusion or romantic preconception, he could never get over the feeling of loss which ensued from the inevitable victory of experience. So, too, with Hemingway whose light of the world is an illusion of happiness or goodness and whose character Paco, for example, has the good fortune to die with all his illusions intact. Yet all of these American writers, all of them of the first rank, never deny the value of experience. If it is bitter, it is still bitterly necessary. Hawthorne's Robin must leave the paradisal grove of his too innocent home. Melville's Redburn and Captain Delano must learn what they can of evil. Twain's cub pilot must learn the face of the river. Hemingway's Nick Adams cannot possibly keep his illusions intact.

Yet perhaps I too enthusiastically refer these similar dilemmas to transcendentalism. The dilemmas originate certainly in the nature of American life, with its queer insistence on some idealism which is usually called the American dream and with its equal insistence on "facts" and performance. Sean O'Faolain once wrote: "At Harvard I learned most uncomfortably that facts are facts. In Italy I learned that facts are the way you look at them." But had that wonderful Irishman stayed with us longer he might have found that we are as much Pirandellos as we are Gradgrinds, that even at Harvard there are relativists. That, indeed, Harvard produced and fostered the relativistic philosophy of pragmatism. It should not have been called "pragmatism," for in the words of its best spokesman, William James, pragmatism involved other matters than facts. "Facts are good, of course," he wrote, "give us lots of facts. Principles are good—give us plenty of principles. The world is indubitably one if you look at it in one way, but as indubitably is it many, if you look at it in another." And, "I offer the oddly-named thing pragmatism as a philosophy that . . . can remain religious like the rationalisms, but at the same time, like the empiricisms, it can preserve the richest intimacy with facts." Now, Frost, too, preserves the richest intimacy with facts without feeling that he must give up comity with religion, rationalism or monism. He can be both a relativist and an absolutist. Perhaps, however, he feels a stronger pull at the seams than did William James. Most of his poems stop short of any final commitment and are content to play off fact against the way-you-look-at-facts. Surely, one must see all the play of fantasy—the elves, lonely boys bending birch trees—as the emergence of the human point of view which softens the fact of the faceless ground swell or the voiceless ice storm?

But Frost's best poems move a step beyond; fact and fantasy are played off against each other for a purpose or at least with a result. The result is, if not a defined or developed philosophy, a sensuous perception of a rationalistic monism— in a word "absolutism." I can think of no poem which so well demonstrates this relationship than one which is certainly among Frost's best and the one which I happen to prefer among them all, "West-Running Brook."

A newly married couple observe that a brook runs west, contrary to the direction of "all the other country brooks" flowing "east to reach the ocean." The wife represents the voice of fantasy, wishful thinking. Like the bird in "The Wood-Pile," she takes the brook "as personal":

> 'As you and I are married to each other,
> We'll both be married to the brook. We'll build
> Our bridge across it, and the bridge shall be
> Our arm thrown over it asleep beside it.
> Look, look, it's waving to us with a wave
> To let us know it hears me.'

For a moment the husband speaks for fact. His words to her are jocular, but his parenthetical thoughts are apprehension of the fact. These thoughts are solemn, almost oppressive:

>   'Why, my dear,
> That wave's been standing off this jut of shore—'
> (The black stream, catching on a sunken rock,
> Flung backward on itself in one white wave,
> And the white water rode the black forever,
> Not gaining but not losing, like a bird
> White feathers from the struggle of whose breast
> Flecked the dark steam and flecked the darker pool
> Below the point, and were at last driven wrinkled

[97]

In a white scarf against the far shore alders.)
'That wave's been standing off this jut of shore
Ever since rivers, I was going to say,
Were made in heaven. It wasn't waved to us.'

When the wife insists that it was waved as "an annunciation,"
Fred teases her for her subjectivity:

'Oh, if you take it off to lady-land,
As 'twere the country of the Amazons
We men must see you to the confines of
And leave you there, ourselves forbid to enter,—
It is your brook! I have no more to say.'

And yet from the stirring together of his cognizance of the
fact of the brook with her fantasy, an intuitive awareness of
a unifying principle evolves. And while truth claimed earlier
(in the parenthetic comprehension of the brook as it is) a
solemnity of image and diction, this subsequent appreciation
of unity claims a greater gravity:

'Speaking of contraries, see how the brook
In that white wave runs counter to itself.
It is from that in water we were from
Long, long before we were from any creature.
Here we, in our impatience of the steps,
Get back to the beginning of beginnings,
The stream of everything that runs away.
Some say existence like a Pirouot
And Pirouette, forever in one place,
Stands still and dances, but it runs away,
It seriously, sadly, runs away
To fill the abyss' void with emptiness.
It flows beside us in this water brook,
But it flows over us. It flows between us
To separate us for a panic moment.

It flows between us, over us, and *with* us.
And it is time, strength, tone, light, life, and love—
And even substance lapsing unsubstantial;
The universal cataract of death
That spends to nothingness—and unresisted,
Save by some strange resistance in itself,
Not just a swerving, but a throwing back,
As if regret were in it and were sacred.
It has this throwing backward on itself
So that the fall of most of it is always
Raising a little, sending up a little.
Our life runs down in sending up the clock.
The brook runs down in sending up our life.
The sun runs down in sending up the brook.
And there is something sending up the sun.
It is this backward motion toward the source,
Against the stream, that most we see ourselves in,
The tribute of the current to the source.
It is from this in nature we are from.
It is most us.'

The perception, smelted to its essence, would seem to be that
though everything in nature is running down, everything is
also recreating "a little,/ sending up a little." That, finally,
in the very nature of the drift to nothingness, there exists a
counter drift (the fact that it is quantitatively smaller does not
alter the picture) toward renewal. Even the brook which runs
counter to the usual direction contains a wave running counter
to the brook itself. That fantasy and truth, that the relative
and the demonstrably true, are components of the final vision
is the insistence of the ending of the poem. The wife says of her
husband's long speech, his observation of contraries, "Today
will be the day/ You said so." He replies, "No, today will be
the day / You said the brook was called West-running Brook."
The final words of the poem are the wife's. She retains and

enlarges her point of view: "Today will be the day of what we both said."

I came to "West-Running Brook" by way of a reference to William James. The poem might well be read in conjunction with a letter and two postcards that James wrote to Henry Adams in 1910. James is considering Adams' well-known analogy between history, which he saw as continuously running down, and the second law of thermodynamics. Here are James's words.

Bad-Nauheim, June 17, 1910

Dear Henry Adams,—I have been so "slim" since seeing you, and the baths here have so weakened my brain, that I have been unable to do any reading except trash, and have only just got round to finishing your "letter," which I had but half-read when I was with you at Paris. To tell the truth, it doesn't impress me at all, save by its wit and erudition; and I ask you whether an old man soon about to meet his Maker can hope to save himself from the consequences of his life by pointing to the wit and learning he has shown in treating a tragic subject.

No, sir, you can't do it, can't impress God in that way. So far as our scientific conceptions go, it may be admitted that your Creator (and mine) started the universe with a certain amount of "energy" latent in it, and decreed that everything that should happen thereafter should be a result of parts of that energy falling to lower levels; raising other parts higher, to be sure, in so doing, but never in equivalent amount, owing to the constant radiation of unrecoverable warmth incidental to the process. It is customary for gentlemen to pretend to believe one another, and until some one hits upon a newer revolutionary concept (which may be tomorrow) all physicists must play the game by holding religiously to the above doctrine. It involves of course the ultimate cessation of all perceptible happening, and the end of human history. With this general conception as *surrounding* everything you say in your "letter," no one can find any fault—in the present stage of scientific conventions and fashions. But I protest against your interpretation of some of the specifications of the great statistical drift downwards of the original high-level energy. If, instead of criticising what you seem to me to say, I express my own interpretation dogmatically, and leave you to make the comparison, it will doubtless conduce to brevity and economize recrimination.

To begin with, the *amount* of cosmic energy it costs to buy a certain distribution of fact which humanly we regard as precious, seems to me to be an altogether secondary matter as regards the question of history and progress. Certain arrangements of matter *on the same energy-level* are, from the point of view of man's appreciation, superior, while others are inferior. Physically a dinosaur's brain may show as much intensity of energy-exchange as a man's, but it can do infinitely fewer things, because as a force of detent it can only unlock the dinosaur's muscles, while the man's brain, by unlocking far feebler muscles, indirectly can by their means issue proclamations, write books, describe Chartres Cathedral, etc., and guide the energies of the shrinking sun into channels which never would have been entered otherwise—in short, *make* history. Therefore the man's brain and muscles are, from the point of view of the historian, the more important place of energy-exchange, small as this may be when measured in absolute physical units.

The "second law" is wholly irrelevant to "history"—save that it sets a terminus—for history is the course of things before that terminus, and all that the second law says is that, whatever the history, it must invest itself between that initial maximum and that terminal minimum of difference in energy-level. As the great irrigation-reservoir empties itself, the whole question for us is that of the distribution of its effects, of *which* rills to guide it into; and the size of the rills has nothing to do with their significance. Human cerebration is the most important rill we know of, and both the

[101]

"capacity" and the "intensity" factor thereof may be treated as infinitesimal. Yet the filling of such rills would be cheaply bought by the waste of whole sums spent in getting a little of down-flowing torrent to enter them. . . .

The first of the postcards is dated June 19, 1910:

P.S. Another illustration of my meaning: The clock of the universe is running down, and by so doing makes the hands move. The energy absorbed by the hands and the *mechanical* work they do is the same day after day, no matter how far the weights have descended from the position they were originally wound up to. The *history* which the hands perpetrate has nothing to do with the *quantity* of this work, but follows the *significance* of the figures which they cover on the dial. If they move from O to XII, there is "progress," if from XII to O, there is "decay," etc. etc.

And the second postcard, dated June 26, 1910:

Yours of the 20th, just arriving, pleases me by its docility of spirit and passive subjection to philosophic opinion. Never, never pretend to an opinion of your own! that way lies every annoyance and madness! You tempt me to offer you another illustration— that of the *hydraulic ram* (thrown back to me in an exam. as a "hydraulic goat" by an insufficiently intelligent student). Let this arrangement of metal, placed in the course of a brook, symbolize the machine of human life. It works, clap, clap, clap, day and night, so long as the brook runs *at all*, and no matter how full the brook (which symbolizes the descending cosmic energy) may be, it works always to the same effect, of raising so many kilogrammeters of water. What the *value* of this work as history may be, depends on the uses to which the water is put in the house which the ram serves.

Not only does the correspondence illuminate the philosophic

problem in "West-Running Brook" but it almost too dramatically, too mysteriously turns to the same images—the clock,
the brook, and the hydraulic ram which operates much as the
wave operates in the poem. I do not know if Frost ever read
James's correspondence. In any case, the worth of the parallel
seems to me to lie in the bright coincidence which brings two
superb sensibilities from different times and fields into line
with each other in such a way as to be in line also with the
more general or average experience. This is what it means to
speak for the many, to draw from the half-realized attitudes
of a generation or a century the notions which like heavy clouds
move and merge in ponderous confusion, and to give them
phrase, form, and above all image. I look, then, on James's
letters and Frost's poem as co-ordinates in a course charted
through a universe of Einsteinian relativity. Co-ordinates in
the sense that they try to give us points about which we assume
a "beginning," an "establishedness," a quasi absolute from
which to measure. Both consider the very great grounds for
skepticism. They must even allow the validity of these grounds.
What else can a person of intelligence do? Yet they both insist
upon first the human point of view and make this view into
a factor in the equation. Perhaps the answer is not greatly
altered by the addition, but it is changed. What is true relative
to nature is confronted by what is relative to human aspiration,
and the result is a grasping for a principle which will be true
to both. Specifically, Frost's poem, like James's letters, says,
yes, the fires of the universe may be burning out and our lives
may be running down, but that very detritus is a form of
energy, a movement which can create other things and which,
therefore, apes the origin of all things. The poem worships,
in other words, the God which science imposes upon the consciousness of modern man. "West-Running Brook," then, is
a poem which moves through irresponsible whimsy, bleak
pluralism, skepticism, and irreligion to monism and a guarded
faith, without ever discarding any of the philosophic or psychological opposites or doubts.

[103]

Though "West-Running Brook" is for me the summit of Frost's poetry, there remain some lesser poems which serve as affirmative footnotes. The clock image, somewhat metamorphosed, appears in an earlier poem, "I Will Sing You One-O." The poem begins in a moment of doubt. The poet has lain awake in a snowy night uncertain as to the time. Then a tower clock strikes "One!" And other clocks murmur the note among themselves:

> In that grave One
> They spoke of the sun
> And moon and stars,
> Saturn and Mars
> And Jupiter.
> Still more unfettered,
> They left the named
> And spoke of the lettered,
> The sigmas and taus
> Of constellations.
> They filled their throats
> With the furthest bodies
> To which man sends his
> Speculation,
> Beyond which God is;
> The cosmic motes
> Of yawning lenses.
> Their solemn peal
> Were not their own:
> They spoke for the clock
> With whose vast wheels
> Theirs interlock.

I do not imply that the God-clock in this poem is identical with the clock "our lives send up" in "West-Running Brook," but in this poem, dedicated to seeking out a first cause, the clock appears. And if the brook image is reminiscent of Emerson and Hawthorne, the clock ought to remind one of the horological sermon in Melville's *Pierre*. The title itself, "I Will Sing You One-O," though evidently derived from the old Crusades' song, puns toward this same quasi absolutism.

An essentially similar formulation, clouded by an obscurant fatigue, characterizes the relatively late poem "Too Anxious for Rivers." The river, evidently symbolic, runs "into the canyon / Of Ceasing to Question What Doesn't Concern Us," which by keeping us from going out "too far in the distance" may be thought a "mercy." A gloomy and rather American-Puritan beginning. But it finishes:

> The world as we know is an elephant's howdah;
> The elephant stands on the back of a turtle;
> The turtle in turn on a rock in the ocean.
> And how much longer a story has science
> Before she must put out the light on the children
> And tell them the rest of the story is dreaming?
> 'You children may dream it and tell it tomorrow.'
> Time was we were molten, time was we were vapor.
> What set us on fire and what set us revolving
> Lucretius the Epicurean might tell us
> 'Twas something we knew all about to begin with
> And needn't have fared into space like his master
> To find 'twas the effort, the essay of love.

Obviously, the poem shares ground with those poems which suffer from a failure of nerve superimposed upon a chubby complacency. Yet "the essay of love." This tells us much. The essay of love contradicts doubt and relativism. Something more, too. For finally we must see that at the heart of Frost's dislike of fanatic political change, of philosophic quarrels, is a distrust of the relativism which appears in his own poems disguised and disarmed as fantasy. However, he never takes his own fantasy seriously, whereas he sees others everywhere tacking with the careless wind, following the brief intellectual fashion with intense seriousness. It is not that Frost in "The Bear" feels contempt for Aristotle or Plato but that he is amused by man's shuttling back and forth between metaphysical extremes. Not that Frost himself may not in a trivial poem also pursue a limited or subjective satisfaction. But in his better self and in his better poems he refuses to play the caitiff of time and yields to the vision which appears in the words of God in "A Masque of Reason":

> My forte is truth,
> Or metaphysics, long the world's reproach
> For standing still in one place true forever;
> While science goes self-superseding on.
> Look at how far we've left the current science
> Of Genesis behind. The wisdom there though,
> Is just as good as when I uttered it.
> Still, novelty has doubtless an attraction.

God, the beginning and end, the absolute principle and unity, stands in the center. Yet it is not for this vision that we should honor Frost's poetry. A belief in the permanency of God is not hard to assert. Rather, we must honor his poems for the difficulty by which he attains the vision.

Frost has been prey to common distractions. He has written at a time when the choice for the poet seemed to lie among the forms of despair: Science, solipsism, or the religion of a past century. And other poets of stature have made their singular choice of the perishing republic or the ideas of order or the cultivation of Christmas trees. Frost has refused all of these and in the refusal has long seemed less dramatically committed than others. He has seemed a nature poet, a spokesman for New England. But no, he must be seen as dramatically uncommitted to the single solution. Like William James he refuses to deny either facts or principles. But he has lived deeply into the century which James only touched, and he would never say as James said to Royce, "Damn the absolute." He has lived into a century which has ceased to try to kill religion by science or science by religion or—worst of all—to convert them into bosom friends. He has lived into a century in which science has presented us with a finite universe but which has become aware that a finite universe does not prescribe a finite God. Insofar as Frost allows to both fact and intuition a bright kingdom, he speaks for many of us. Insofar as he speaks through an amalgam of senses and sure experience so that his poetry seems a nostalgic memory with overtones touching some conceivable future, he speaks better than most of us. That is to say, as a poet must.

A Chronology

1874	Born, March 26, in San Francisco, California. Son of William Prescott Frost, Jr., and Isabelle Moodie Frost.
1874–85	Early years in San Francisco.
1885	Moves after the death of his father to Lawrence, Massachusetts, with mother and sister.
1892	Graduates from Lawrence High School. Brief attendance at Dartmouth College.
1895	Marries Elinor Miriam White, who had been co-valedictorian with Frost at Lawrence High School.
1896	Birth of son, Eliot.
1897–99	Undergraduate at Harvard University.
1899	Birth of daughter, Lesley.
1900–1910	Farming near West Derry, New Hampshire. Teaching at Pinkerton Academy, Derry Village.
1900	Birth of son, Carol. Death of son, Eliot.
1903	Birth of daughter, Irma.
1905	Birth of daughter, Marjorie.
1907	Birth of daughter, Elinor Bettina, who died in infancy.
1911–12	Teacher at New Hampshire State Normal School, Plymouth, New Hampshire.
1912–15	Sojourn in England with wife and four children. Farming in Buckinghamshire and Herefordshire.
1913	*A Boy's Will*.
1914	*North of Boston*.

1915	Returns to America as an established poet. Farms near Franconia, New Hampshire.
1916	*Mountain Interval.*
	Elected to National Institute of Arts and Letters.
1917–20	Professor of English, Amherst College.
1919	Moves to new farm, South Shaftsbury, Vermont.
1920	Helps to found Bread Loaf School of English, Middlebury College.
1921–23	Poet in Residence, University of Michigan.
1923	*New Hampshire.*
	Selected Poems.
1923–25	Professor of English, Amherst College.
1924	Pulitzer Prize for *New Hampshire.*
1925–26	Fellow in Letters, University of Michigan.
1926–38	Professor of English, Amherst College.
1928	*West-Running Brook.*
1930	*Collected Poems.*
1931	Pulitzer Prize for *Collected Poems.*
1933	Litt. D. at Dartmouth College.
1934	Death of Marjorie Frost Fraser.
1936	*A Further Range.*
	Charles Eliot Norton Professor of Poetry, Harvard University.
1937	Pulitzer Prize for *A Further Range.*
	Litt. D. at Harvard University.
1938	Death of Elinor White Frost.
1939	*Collected Poems.*
1939–42	Ralph Waldo Emerson Fellow in Poetry, Harvard University.
1940	Death of Carol Frost.
1942	*A Witness Tree.*
1943	Pulitzer Prize for *A Witness Tree.*

1943–49	Ticknor Fellow in the Humanities, Dartmouth College.
1945	*A Masque of Reason.*
1947	*Steeple Bush.*
	A Masque of Mercy.
1948	Litt. D. at Amherst College.
1949	*Complete Poems.*
1952	Litt. D. at Durham University, Durham, England.
1957	Litt. D.'s at Oxford and Cambridge universities and at National University of Ireland.
1958	Consultant in Poetry to Library of Congress.
1961	Reads "The Gift Outright" at presidential inauguration.
	Trip to Israel as guest of the Hebrew University.
1962	*In the Clearing.*
	LL. D. at the University of Michigan.
	Trip to Russia as guest of the Soviet Government.
1963	Awarded the Bollingen Prize.

Selective Bibliography

Works by Robert [Lee] Frost

Twilight. Lawrence, Massachusetts: Privately printed, 1894.

A Boy's Will. London: Nutt, 1913; New York: Holt, 1915.

North of Boston. London: Nutt, 1914; New York: Holt, 1915.

Mountain Interval. New York: Holt, 1916

A Way Out. New York: The Harbor Press, 1929. First printed in 1917.

New Hampshire: A Poem with Notes and Grace Notes. New York: Holt, 1923.

Selected Poems. New York: Holt, 1923.

West-Running Brook. New York: Holt, 1928.

Selected Poems, rev. ed. New York: Holt, 1928.

Collected Poems of Robert Frost. New York: Holt, 1930.

A Further Range. New York: Holt, 1936.

Collected Poems of Robert Frost: 1939. New York: Holt, 1939.

A Witness Tree. New York: Holt, 1942.

A Masque of Reason. New York: Holt, 1945.

The Poems of Robert Frost. New York: Modern Library Edition, 1946.

A Masque of Mercy. New York: Holt, 1947.

Steeple Bush. New York: Holt, 1947.

Complete Poems of Robert Frost: 1949. New York: Holt, 1949.

In the Clearing. New York: Holt, Rinehart and Winston, 1962.

Books and Articles about Frost

Cook, Reginald L., *The Dimensions of Robert Frost.* New York: Rinehart, 1958.

Cox, James M., ed., *Robert Frost: A Collection of Critical Essays.* Englewood Cliffs, New Jersey: Prentice-Hall, 1962.

Cox, Sidney, *A Swinger of Birches: A Portrait of Robert Frost.* New York: New York Univ. Press, 1957.

Greenberg, Robert A. and James G. Hepburn, eds., *Robert Frost: An Introduction.* New York: Holt, Rinehart and Winston, 1961.

Jarrell, Randall, "The Other Robert Frost" and "To the Laodiceans" in *Poetry and the Age.* New York: Knopf, 1953, pp. 28–69.

Lynen, John F., *The Pastoral Art of Robert Frost.* New Haven: Yale Univ. Press, 1960.

Munson, Gorham B., *Robert Frost: A Study in Sensibility and Good Sense.* New York: George H. Doran, 1927.

Nitchie, George W., *Human Values in the Poetry of Robert Frost.* Durham: Duke Univ. Press, 1960.

Pineda, Rafael, *Robert Frost en los bosques de Nueva Inglaterra.* Valencia: Universidad de Carabobo, 1960. Contains translations into Spanish of some of Frost's poems.

Poirier, Richard, "The Art of Poetry II: Robert Frost" [An interview with Robert Frost], *The Paris Review,* 6 (Summer-Fall 1960), 89–120.

Sergeant, Elizabeth Shepley, *Robert Frost: The Trial by Existence.* New York: Holt, Rinehart and Winston, 1960.

Thompson, Lawrance, *Fire and Ice: The Art and Thought of Robert Frost.* New York: Holt, 1942.

—— *Robert Frost.* Minneapolis: Univ. of Minnesota Press, 1959. (Univ. of Minnesota Pamphlets on American Writers, no. 2.)

Trilling, Lionel, "A Speech on Robert Frost: A Cultural Episode," *Partisan Review,* 26 (Summer 1959), 445–52.

Waggoner, Hyatt Howe, "The Humanistic Idealism of Robert Frost," *American Literature,* 13 (November 1941), 207–33.

Warren, Robert Penn, "The Themes of Robert Frost" in *The*

Writer and His Craft: Being the Hopwood Lectures 1932–1952. Ann Arbor: The Univ. of Michigan Press, 1954, pp. 218–33.

Watts, Harold H., "Robert Frost and the Interrupted Dialogue," *American Literature,* 27 (March 1955), 69–87.

Winters, Yvor, "Robert Frost: Or the Spiritual Drifter as Poet," *Sewanee Review,* 56 (August 1948), 564–96.

Index

63 45976

SEP 3 0 1963 DATE DUE

MAY 1 9 1967			
MAY 6 1981			

100M—3-63—53284—Ark.P.&L.Co.